WHAT TO DO WHEN THE IRS COMES CALLING

E. Dennis Bridges, CPA

Copyright © 2016 E. Dennis Bridges

All rights reserved.

DEDICATION

Dedicated to my wife, Robin, who has encouraged me every step of the way.

And to my two incredible daughters, Katherine and Kimberly, who are my inspiration every day that I live.

Collectively, you are the joy of my life, and my reason for living.

I love you all more than words can say.

Important Notice

While every effort has been taken to ensure that the information contained herein is accurate as of the time of publication, tax laws and regulations are constantly changing.

This book is designed to provide accurate and authoritative information in regards to the subject matter covered, but it is sold with the understanding that the publisher is not engaged in rendering legal, accounting, or other professional services, and no information contained herein should be construed as legal advice.

If legal advice or other expert assistance is required, the services of a competent professional person should be sought. The publisher does not guarantee or warrant that readers who use the information provided in this publication will achieve results similar to those discussed.

If you are in need of professional tax assistance, such as in the event of an audit, collections action, or other IRS matter, it is highly suggested that you contact the author directly at **(770) 984-8008.**

CONTENTS

Introduction 3

CHAPTER 1   Where It All Started 5

CHAPTER 2   Don't Let This Happen To You 9

CHAPTER 3   Determining When You Need Professional Assistance 13

CHAPTER 4   Minimizing Your Tax Bill: It All Starts With Your Tax Returns 23

CHAPTER 5   Four Heavy-Duty, Tax-Cutting, Money-Saving Secrets the IRS Doesn't Want You To Know 37

CHAPTER 6   Understanding IRS Collections And The Resolution Process. 55

CHAPTER 7   Government Rubber Glove: The IRS Financial Probe 63

CHAPTER 8   Snatching Victory From The Jaws of Defeat 75

CHAPTER 9   Tax Debt Resolution Options 81

CHAPTER 10   Time: It's Either On Your Side Or Their's (OK, Just Theirs) .. 89

CHAPTER 11   Ill-Gotten Gains 95

CHAPTER 12   Nasty Things The IRS Can Do To You: Liens, Levies And Wage Garnishments 97

CHAPTER 13   My Favorite Client, Everett Suters 109

CHAPTER 14   "Regrets, I've Had Few…" 113

About The Author 115

INTRODUCTION

Without a doubt, the Internal Revenue Service (IRS) is at once the most hated and most feared of all U.S. government agencies. They have the seeming power to make grown men quake in their boots, and turn reasonably sane adults into masses of quivering jelly.

The thought of receiving <u>ANY</u> letter from the IRS – anything except a refund check – makes normal men and women break out in a sweat.

For most of the past 30 years, my practice, based in Atlanta, has focused on providing relief to taxpayers across the U.S. to help them overcome severe IRS problems.

Honestly, there isn't a lot we haven't seen, both in terms of client situations and IRS actions.

Having just celebrated 30 years of being in practice, my thoughts are mostly with the wonderful relationships with friends and clients with which we have been blessed.

And at the same time, even though I see changes in IRS procedures, the fact remains that most U.S. taxpayers, especially those that owe delinquent taxes, are paralyzed over the prospect of enforced collection action. But, we'll get to that later.

So with that background, my over-arching goal in writing this book is to level the playing field in dealing with the IRS in two specific situations: When you owe money to IRS that you can't pay, and also in dealing with those dreaded tax audits. To help your wallet, we'll also cover a few of the most valuable tax-cutting strategies available.

For good measure, I'm including a sprinkling of my most rewarding and memorable cases from the past 30 years.

Over the years, it has been a privilege to assist and represent some of the finest, salt-of-the-earth people I have ever met in the wide spectrum of transportation industries. We've assisted truck drivers, airline pilots, couriers, and Uber drivers. So as a special bonus, we are adding a bonus section with the tax-cutting, money-saving guidance for individuals in many of these areas.

My mission — my passion, if you will — is to give America's taxpayers a fighting chance against the most feared and reviled government agency in the United States. If I can help you sleep just a little better, and help you find some measure of control, then we have reached our goal.

Happy Tax-cutting!

E. Dennis Bridges, CPA

Atlanta, Georgia

September 1, 2016

CHAPTER 1

WHERE IT ALL STARTED

One of my greatest pleasures over the past 15 years or so has been getting to travel across the country and speak to industry groups, as well as groups of CPAs and attorneys that do the same thing I do. The real fun has been with the people I've been privileged to meet.

Very often, after I've finished with my prepared talk, I'll take several questions, which usually are tax-related. The real fun is getting to visit with folks one-on-one, either at a reception after the event or casually in a bar over a club soda. Interestingly, one of the questions I'm asked most frequently is, "What is it that gives you the passion for what you do?"

Honestly, it probably has a lot to do with how I grew up. There wasn't a lot of money to go around in those days, and therein were the seeds planted.

If I wanted something, the usual answer was, "We can't afford it." At Christmas, I didn't get what I wanted, I got what I needed, which usually was socks and underwear. (Of all things, if one of my daughters asks me now what I want for Christmas, I usually say, "socks and underwear!")

-Flashback-

We were on a "day trip" at the time. The year was probably 1966, so I would have been about twelve years old. There wasn't a lot of money in those days, so a vacation for us consisted of a day visit to some random attraction, maybe 50 or 60 miles away.

My dad had noticed that my eyes would light up every time I saw a big 18-wheeler come along and pass us. "You want to have some fun?" he asked me. I was afraid it was one of those "pull my finger" jokes that he was famous for, but I was bored, so I went along.

He said "Next time one of those big trucks comes along, roll down the window and stick out your arm, and pump it like this," making an air horn motion.

In less than two minutes, another big truck appeared off in the distance behind us.

My heart raced immediately with anticipation.

When the truck was maybe 500 yards from us, I rolled the window down and stuck my head out the window.

(You can tell this was a hundred years ago, 'cause the windows "rolled down!")

We were in the left lane, and the huge 18-wheeler was coming up on the right. I was half hanging out of the window, my hair blowing like crazy in the wind.

When the giant truck was almost up with us, I summoned the courage to do what my dad had said, and I started pumping my arm like an air horn. The truck slowed down, and the driver obligingly gave me several friendly pulls on his air horn.

Wow! He did that just for me, I thought!

But that wasn't even the best part…

As he edged closer and was even with our car, he looked down from his cabover tractor, and with a warm smile, he waved at me.

O-M-G! I was in heaven!

Seriously, the whole rest of the day of our trip, I was walking on clouds.

Thus began my love affair with trucking, logistics, and how our economy works.

-End Flashback-

I will forever be grateful for the privilege of growing up in a loving home. But our lack in those days fostered in me a white-hot desire to be able to help individuals and families be able to achieve their financial goals.

In the world of dealing with severe IRS problems, there's little we haven't seen.

Occasionally, when we talk or meet with a client that has a particularly "messy" situation, they will invariably say, "This surely must be the biggest mess you've ever seen." Hopefully, it provides a measure of comfort when I tell them truthfully, "Not even close— we've dealt with some pretty ugly and severe situations in our 30 years of practice."

To be sure, this book is not about me or even about my practice. It's about you and letting you know that there is a solution for your tax problems, no matter how bad you think it might be.

Or, if you simply want to do everything you can to cut your income taxes as much as legally possible every year, we've got your solution there as well.

One of the questions that we get very frequently is, what is it that makes us different from other CPAs, enrolled agents, or attorneys that deal with IRS problems and with tax-cutting strategies?

The short answer is simple: We think outside the box. We love it when other practitioners refer cases to us in which they don't see a happy or viable solution.

Our creative approach didn't come about overnight, and nobody waved their Harry Potter magic wand at me, making me the official "tax wizard."

Over the course of my career, I've had the privilege of being mentored by three of the foremost authorities in the U.S. in the area of IRS practice. One is Robert Shreibman, a tax attorney from Torrance, California, just outside Los Angeles. He had a very gracious secretary years ago, Jane Subeck, who told me he had taken a special interest in me and in "bringing me along." I suspect the truth was that he just felt sorry for me with the sometimes constant questions, with which I would nag him back in the early days. Mr. Shreibman has been a law school professor, author, speaker, and defender in numerous high profile cases over the years.

Another is Jim Wilson, a practitioner and lecturer out of Indianapolis, a man of true wisdom and brilliance. A few years ago, I was speaking at a conference of about 200 attorneys and CPAs in Denver. In the middle of my presentation, I glanced out into the audience, and there was Jim Wilson about ten rows back. He should have been the speaker and I the listener.

More recently, my dear friend and colleague, Jassen Bowman, has been an incredible encouragement to me towards the end of providing serious relief to a broader reach of encumbered and sleepless taxpayers throughout the country. Jassen is both a technical and technological marvel, and I stand grateful for his guidance and contributions in both venues.

Let's jump in now and see how the IRS machine works, and specifically what can be done when they scare the living daylights out of taxpayers all over the country.

CHAPTER 2

DON'T LET THIS HAPPEN TO YOU

Let's start with a quick story…

Human nature being what it is, we tend to put off unpleasant stuff as long as possible.

Hey, I totally get that—I'm a human too. Say you've got a toothache…ugh! You put off going to the dentist 'cause it's gonna cost money. Perfectly good money that you were going to put towards that new fishing boat that you've had your eye on down at Bass Pro Shops.

Blasted!

You know there's gonna be drillin'…and pain. Even with Novocaine!

So you put it off… And you put it off again.

We actually have cases like these all the time, but one case sticks out in particular.

A fellow that owned a photography studio was referred to us by his attorney. Since he was only 60 miles south of Atlanta, he and his wife made an appointment to come in.

We met with them—a very nice couple actually. Seems he owed about $60,000 in payroll taxes.

We got a good clear picture of the IRS situation as well as an initial "snapshot" of their financial picture. They signed a Power of Attorney, and we expected to hear from them within a few days.

We sent them a letter thanking them for coming in. We re-stated the quotes we had talked about and told them we looked forward to getting to work with them in the days ahead.

Those days turned into weeks, which turned into months. We know now that he continued to receive IRS notices, each one more threatening than the last. Each time he received a letter, his wife asked him if he had gotten all of this worked out with our office. Not wanting to worry or scare his wife, he told her, "Yes, honey, I've got it all taken care of."

Then one fateful Friday morning, there's a knock at their door. The wife answers it. Standing there was the Agent in Charge, along with about four other IRS agents and several sheriff's deputies.

One of them is holding the roll of yellow "POLICE" tape that they have already wrapped around the front of their property.

She yells her husband's name at the top of her lungs.

The Agent in Charge informs them that they are conducting a Seizure of Property, and asks them to stand aside while they come in and secure the premises.

The husband quietly tells the Agent that he had been in our office, and would she (the Special Agent) mind if he tries to reach us real quick.

She agrees.

He reaches our office, they got me on the line, and he tells me what is going on with the seizure.

I asked him if he got the name of the Revenue Officer in Charge. He did, and he gave me her name.

I asked him if he would ask her to come to the phone.

Luckily, I had met this agent just a few weeks before under more pleasant circumstances. It was during tax season, and I was partially responsible for organizing a televised call-in program for taxpayers to call in and have either a CPA or IRS agent answer their questions. This was the IRS agent that we had selected for the call-in program.

After a bit of going back and forth, the Agent agreed to a very brief delay in the seizure, and put him on a very short leash to provide us with the information needed to work out a settlement.

We were able to work out an agreeable arrangement, but about three weeks later, I got a call from the Agent that had been in charge of the seizure.

I'm thinking, "Holy smokes—what could she want? Has something gone wrong?"

When I got on the phone, the Agent greeted me graciously, and I nervously responded in kind.

She was calling to commend me for the way that we handled the seizure, adding that those events don't normally have happy endings.

Towards the end of our conversation, she chuckled and said she almost felt sorry for the husband, because it was very clear from the moment his wife answered the door that he was in a lot more trouble with his wife than his was with the IRS!

Primary take away: *Keep your CPA on speed dial!*

CHAPTER 3

DETERMINING WHEN YOU NEED PROFESSIONAL ASSISTANCE

You always have the option of representing yourself in front of the IRS and that is, after all, why you're reading this book. However, many times you may find dealing with the IRS to be frustrating, time consuming, intimidating, or all of the above.

Representing yourself in your tax challenges might sound like an easy way to save a lot of money for yourself, and depending on your situation, this might be true. Unfortunately, I lost count years ago of the number of times that a person said something to the IRS that actually got them further in the hole.

Here are just some of the disadvantages to you representing yourself in front of the IRS:

1. You do not have the professional expertise or know what the options are or how to get the lowest settlement allowed by law.

2. Four out of every five Offers in Compromise submitted by taxpayers are rejected by the IRS. Knowing how to become one of the 20% that is accepted by the IRS can be very, very valuable.

3. Many times when you represent yourself in front of the IRS and obtain an Offer in Compromise, the amount of your Offer in Compromise is much more than is actually required by law. (Hint: It's about *contingent expenses*.)

4. You may end up being too frightened, frustrated or intimidated by the IRS to effectively or comfortably negotiate a settlement. Remember, IRS collections personnel are exactly that: They are professional collections agents.

5. Most taxpayers are far happier to keep their distance from the IRS and prefer to leave the sparring to their advisors. Dealing with the IRS is not always as painful as you may imagine though. In fact there some IRS officers that are reasonable and helpful, particularly when they see that you're making an offers honest effort to resolve your tax problems and pay back what you owe.

6. Unfortunately, you may slip up and inadvertently make statements that can make the problem worse, perhaps triggering an audit, increasing your tax liability, or even a criminal investigation. Never forget that the IRS has their own law enforcement officers.

7. There are things that *you know* that the IRS or your tax representative does not know. If you contact the IRS and are asked about those 'things,' you must answer truthfully, or again, criminal prosecution may result. But if your tax representative doesn't know then in all honesty he or she can answer "I don't know..." A good representative is going to limit his scope of knowledge about you until the appropriate time.

8. Professionals know where to draw the line. You may sometimes make statements that can create tax liability for a business associate, your spouse or someone else.

9. Negotiating with the IRS takes valuable time away from your work and family to wrestle with your own case. Working professionals will do appreciably better paying a tax professional while they more profitably ply their own occupations.

How to Select the Best Tax Consulting Firm

When choosing a firm that will represent you before the IRS, it's important that you know that they are dealing with a professional who is well versed in tax law and IRS procedures. You don't want the IRS to think you're a clown, after all.

IRS representation is a very complicated field with many different laws to interpret. While any attorney, CPA or Enrolled Agent may represent clients before the IRS, few are truly qualified to provide the knowledge, experience and negotiating skills needed to successfully represent you in front of the IRS.

The way I look at it, it is similar to a divorce, bankruptcy, or a criminal trial. Attorneys have different specializations. For example, would you hire a real estate attorney to represent you in a criminal proceeding? Or look at it in the other way, would you want a criminal defense attorney handling your divorce or bankruptcy? Most of the time, the answer is a gigantic, emphatic NO because that is outside that attorney's area of specialization.

As a rule, a firm should have a solid tax resolution track record, which is the best objective indicator of how that firm will manage your case. Here are some key questions that you need to ask before selecting a tax resolution firm:

1. How many years has the firm been in business?
2. Is everybody that would be working on your case licensed?
3. Does the firm discuss all options available to you to resolve you tax problem?
4. What is the firm's success rate?
5. What is the firm's rating with the Better Business Bureau?

Here are some areas of concern to be careful of:

- Beware of unlicensed telemarketers. They're paid on a commission basis for bringing your business to their firm, and these unlicensed sales people are exactly that – *sales people*. When it comes to tax law, these individuals don't know their hind end from an overheating radiator.

- Be especially aware of unrealistic promises or improbable results declared by sales representatives. You want to be sure that you receive top quality work and that you get the services that you actually pay for. If you do some Google searches about certain firms, you'll quickly discover that this is a common complaint against many tax resolution firms.

- Beware of firms that charge you a fee based exclusively on the amount of money that you owe the IRS. Usually the same procedural steps are required to solve both large and small tax obligations. If the firm is quoting you a flat fee for services, ask for a breakdown of exactly what specific services every dollar of the fee quote covers.

- Ask the firm direct questions about your case. If the firm is evasive or their answer seems intentionally complex, it is possible they're trying to disguise direct answers to your questions. You deserve straightforward answers.

- Do not make emotional decisions. When you decide to hire a tax resolution specialty firm, you are seeking peace of mind that your problem will be handled and handled properly. Regardless of which firm you hire, you should feel that you are being properly taken care of and your tax problem will be solved for the lowest amount allowed by law.

Attorneys, accountants, CPA's, enrolled agents and former IRS employees may all provide valuable assistance when it comes to traditional tax accounting work. However, they may not have all of the necessary expertise, experience, and negotiating skills to permanently solve your IRS matter. Solving an IRS dispute involves day to day administrative dealings and requires the know-how to manage the maze of IRS protocols as well as having top notch negotiating skills.

For example, consider a former IRS employee that worked exclusively on auditing large corporate tax returns for 20 years. Then, after leaving the IRS, they become an Enrolled Agent by virtue of their IRS employment. This person never worked in IRS Collections, and never handled individual (1040) tax cases.

Is this the person you really want representing you in a 1040 collections matter?

There is most certainly a right answer to that question!

How to Save on Professional Fees

The single greatest advantage of representing yourself in front of the IRS is that you'll save over the fees of a professional, and for many taxpayers this is no small matter. The amount of fees saved may be dwarfed by the actual tax settlement however. In these situations, you might want to look at your overall financial picture to determine how much money you may be leaving on the table if you don't have expert representation.

Tax professional's fees can range up to several hundred dollars per hour for an expert tax resolution specialist in a major city. Many tax consultants won't agree to a fixed fee to handle your case. For example, when filing an Offer in Compromise they are not able to anticipate how many hours will be required to effectively manage the case due to a multitude of unforeseen contingencies, including the reluctance on the part of the IRS to negotiate a final settlement, possible Appeals that may need to be filed, and other potential issues.

Regardless of the fee arrangement, there's a lot you can do to keep your fees to a minimum:

1. Request monthly statements. This could warn you of overcharges or extensive fees you can't afford before they accumulate.

2. Delegate only the critical parts of your case that you can't handle yourself.

3. Cooperate. <u>Get your financial information together quickly and in an orderly fashion.</u> Don't make your professional chase you for the information.

4. Keep communication with your professional to a minimum. Call sparingly, get to the point, and hang up. Remember, you're probably paying by the hour.

Tax Professionals to Consider

In general, you have three options of tax professionals to represent you in front of the IRS. These are attorneys, certified public accountants or enrolled agents. All three of these professionals are allowed by the IRS to directly represent taxpayers. Let's start with attorneys.

An attorney in good standing in a state bar may represent taxpayers on IRS matters. However, this doesn't mean that all lawyers are qualified to handle your IRS problem. Obviously, you need a tax attorney who's not only experienced but has an exceptional track record. An attorney inexperienced with dealing with the IRS or has a poor rating or no rating with the Better Business Bureau will likely provide very little value because they have yet to develop the feel of what the IRS will accept and do. *Most tax problems are not solved in the courtroom but are resolved via administrative procedures.*

It is most likely that your tax matter will be settled out of court, so an attorney's hourly fees and miscellaneous charges are often the most expensive representation alternative available to you. You will want a tax lawyer if the IRS suspects fraud, is threatening criminal prosecution, or if an appeal to tax court is likely. Ultimately, the firm's track record is the best indicator of how your case will be settled.

Next, let's talk about Certified Public Accountants. Less than 1% of all CPA's are in any way qualified to practice in the arena of tax resolution. Most CPA's have had very little exposure to dealing with IRS tax problems. As with attorneys, any CPA is permitted to handle tax resolution cases. However, that by itself is no assurance of their competence. A CPA inexperienced with negotiating or who has a poor rating or no rating with the BBB will likely provide little value because they have yet to develop, again, the feel of what the IRS will accept and what they won't.

Next, let's discuss Enrolled Agents. Enrolled Agents are neither attorneys nor accountants (although a tiny number of them do have law or accounting degrees). Enrolled Agents become so either via by former employment with Internal Revenue Service or by taking a short series of examinations that are specific to tax matters. After passing these fairly straightforward exams (*well, at least by comparison to the CPA exam!*), an individual can apply to become an Enrolled Agent. An Enrolled Agent, however, that is inexperienced with tax resolution and negotiating will again provide little value. Choose an Enrolled Agent licensed directly by the IRS that is experienced in tax resolution negotiation.

How to Find a Tax Professional

Ask your professional advisors. Your accountant or attorney may not excel in tax matters, but may be able to refer you to another professional who does.

Personal Referrals

Do you have a friend or acquaintance who has gone through tax problems with good results? His or her advisor may do equally well for you. Realize that this could be a difficult matter to discuss with your friends and associates because it's similar to bankruptcy. It's not something that people commonly talk about, but opening up about it may help you find much better representation than otherwise.

Professional Associations

Your local bar association, accounting association, or state Enrolled Agents association may have a referral panel. However, their referral does not necessarily ensure competence with IRS tax negotiation.

A major thing to consider when hiring a professional tax negotiator is to consider the chemistry between you and them. You really need a professional who can offer more than just technical competency. You may need empathy and emotional support from your tax advisor. When you battle the IRS, you need a strong ally in every possible way.

Tax Resolution Resource

I aim to provide the best possible service to each and every one of my clients. Because of this, I must limit the number of new clients I can take on at any given time. If you owe the IRS more than $15,000, I would be happy to take a look at your case and discuss whether we would be a good fit for working together. To request a case review, please call my office today at **(770) 984-8008**.

CHAPTER 4

MINIMIZING YOUR TAX BILL: IT ALL STARTS WITH YOUR TAX RETURNS

Penalties and interest are calculated as percentage of your tax liability. Therefore, *the less you owe on your actual tax returns, the less you will owe overall*. Because of this, it's good to know how the tax return process itself works and how to minimize your tax liability.

The majority of this chapter will cover how to minimize taxes on your personal income tax return, but the end of this chapter will include a section on minimizing your liability for other tax types, particularly Form 941 employment taxes for businesses.

Your Personal Income Tax Return (1040)

There are numerous books published every tax season promising you how to keep your tax bill to an absolute minimum, and they want you to buy a new such book every year. The dirty little secret of the "annual tax savings book industry", however, is that their books are usually nothing more than heavily annotated reprinting of IRS Publication 17, which is the IRS handbook for filing a personal income tax return.

These published books, and Pub 17, walk through the entire process of preparing a tax return, including every form, schedule, and worksheet that gets attached to your Form 1040. Publication 17 is available for free from your local IRS office, or you can download a PDF from irs.gov.

My purpose in this chapter is not to go through every bit of Pub 17 and regurgitate it. As I already mentioned, there are plenty of other books out there that have already done that. In this chapter, I want to present the main ideas behind how your tax bill is computed, and what goes into minimizing it.

Income

First, let's look at the one item that has the biggest impact on your personal income tax: Your income. Income has an extremely broad definition in the Internal Revenue Code. Essentially, any time you experience a financial gain of any sort, the government considers it income, with a few limited exceptions.

Money you make from your job, a side business, or any other activity is all income. If you sell stocks, bonds, houses, or any other investments for a gain, that's considered income. If you buy a car on Craigslist, keep it for 6 months, and then sell it to somebody else on Craigslist for more than you paid for it and what you put into it for repairs, then that profit is taxable income.

If you trade services with another person and you get the better end of the deal, the monetary equivalent of that gain is also taxable as income. For example, consider a house painter and his neighbor that is an auto mechanic. The house painter agrees to repaint three rooms in his neighbor's home in exchange for a transmission overhaul on his car that would normally cost $1200. If the painter would normally charge $800 to paint those three rooms, then the painter actually got the better end of the deal and must claim the $400 difference as taxable income.

There are plenty of people that obviously ignore this rule, and you may have done it yourself. Some people even do this as a normal course of doing business, especially with the current job market and economic conditions. People that are used to getting paid in cash, just as bartenders, waiters, piano teachers, figure skating coaches, and numerous other professionals, are particularly at risk of falling into this trap.

I cannot emphasize enough the importance of properly reporting all your income, **<u>especially</u>** if you are already on the IRS radar. One of the most common questions that every tax professional is asked has to do with what factors increase your chances of being audited. While it is true that certain deductions and credits claimed on a tax return create a higher risk of being audited, the absolute single biggest risk factor for being audited for a tax return is *already having a tax problem.*

If you're reading this book, I can only assume that you fall into this high-risk audit category. Since your audit risk is so much higher than everybody else, it behooves you to report all your income on your tax returns to avoid massive penalties, fines, and perhaps even criminal prosecution for tax evasion.

Remember, the law states that you're required to pay your fair share of tax, and **not one penny more**. In the world of tax geeks, I consider myself fairly aggressive when it comes to taking deductions and credits, compared to so many tax practitioners that won't enter into anything that looks like a "gray area". You should take each and every tax break that you're in any way, shape, or form entitled to.

However, you should also still report every penny of income, especially if you're already under IRS scrutiny in any way.

Adjustments

Adjustments to income are those things on the first page of a long form 1040 that are directly deducted from your income. These are deductions that everybody can take, even if you don't itemize deductions (Schedule A). Adjustments to income include things like:

- student loan interest
- moving expenses you paid for taking a job somewhere
- half of your self-employment tax
- classroom expenses paid out of pocket by teachers
- alimony you pay
- tuition and fees
- contributions to Health Savings Accounts
- contributions to some types of retirement accounts

These deductions come directly off your income, and therefore reduce a very critical number in your income tax calculation: **Adjusted Gross Income** (AGI). AGI is a term we will use frequently. Remember, it's just all your income minus the things listed above. If you paid any of these items, make sure you claim them!

Deductions

Deductions are amounts subtracted from your AGI to determine your taxable income. However, deductions, unlike allowances discussed above, are subject to minimum threshold limits. Since every person is given a "standard deduction", your itemized deductions should exceed this standard deduction in order for you to claim it. In addition, some other deductions have their own minimums before you can claim them. For example, medical expenses have to exceed 10.0% of your AGI before you can start to claim them.

Here are the most common itemized deductions to be aware of:

- medical and dental expenses that exceed 10.0% of your AGI
- state and local sales taxes you paid throughout the year
- real estate taxes
- personal property taxes (such as on cars, boats, airplanes, etc.)
- home mortgage interest and points
- mortgage insurance premiums
- interest on investments
- donations to charity
- the value of losses you suffered due to theft or natural disaster

Certain expenses are subject to what is called the 2% floor rule. Like the 10.0% rule for medical expenses indicated above, the sum of other deduction types has to exceed 2% of your AGI before you can claim them. These expenses include things such as:

- expenses you pay for your job that you are not reimbursed for, such as travel, union dues, uniforms, job-related classes, dry cleaning, etc.
- tax preparation fees
- investments expenses
- safety deposit boxes

Remember, it is the sum total of these types of expenses that have to exceed 2% of your AGI, it is NOT 2% for each individual expense. Also remember that it is the amount in excess of 2% of your AGI that you can deduct.

Don't forget, if you're able to claim any of these deductions, and you think they might add up to more than your standard deduction, then CLAIM THEM. Every deduction reduces your taxable income, and therefore your tax bill.

The standard deduction varies depending on your marital status, and the amounts generally go up every year based on inflation. If you are single or married but filing separate returns, you get the lowest standard deduction ($6,300 for 2016 tax returns). If you are single, but eligible to claim head of household status because you take care of another qualifying person (it does not have to be your own child), then you can claim the next highest standard deduction ($9,300 for 2016). If you are married and filing a joint return, you can claim the highest standard deduction ($12,600 for 2016). If you are blind and either you or your spouse exceed the age of 65, you are eligible for special standard deductions.

Your total deductions, whether you take the standard deduction you qualify for or you itemize to get a bigger deduction, is very important. These deductions reduce your taxable income dollar for dollar. As will be discussed later in the chapter on Substitute for Returns, the IRS does not give you anything except the standard deduction for single people if they file a return for you, so you never want them to do this.

Exemptions

While it costs significantly more than $4,050 per year to take care of another person, Congress at least recognizes that it costs *something* to do so. Because of this, you can deduct an additional $4,050 in 2016 for every other person that you can claim an exemption for. Generally, this includes yourself, your spouse, your own kids that you take care of (even if they don't live with you in some circumstances), other relatives you take care, and in some rare cases, even non-relatives you provide for.

The rules covering whom you can claim as a dependent are a bit complex, and each rule has a list of oddball exceptions. All of those rules are beyond the scope of this book, but Publication 17 has a thorough explanation, and we can also help you determine who you can claim and who you can't (just give me a call at 770-984-8008 and we can help you out with this).

What I would like to emphasize to you regarding dependents is this: If you even think you might be able to claim somebody, at least TRY. You may not think that you can claim an exemption for your kid niece that spent a good chunk of the year with you, but you might actually be surprised. Same with your grandparents in the nursing home. Same with your son's best friend that lived with you all year. Same thing with your kids that lived with your ex all year and you never even saw all year.

Most of the rules regarding who can claim who as a dependent come down to the terms of divorce agreements, who spent the money to take care of somebody, how long they lived with you, or who simply has responsibility for the person. Again, try to claim every dependent you can, even if you think you can't – you may just be surprised.

You shouldn't claim a dependent that you legally can't, but if by some weird twist of the complex rules you can claim somebody, then do it.

Like adjustments and deductions, exemptions for dependents reduce your taxable income dollar for dollar. The more exemptions you claim, the lower your tax bill is going to be.

Taxable Income and Tax

Your total income from all sources, minus your adjustments, deductions, and exemptions, equals your **taxable income**. Your taxable income is, as the term implies, the amount of your income that is actually subject to tax.

Personal income taxes in the United States are based on marginal tax rates. What this means is that your tax rate is different for different chunks of your taxable income. For example, a single person's 2016 taxable income is taxed at a rate of 10% on the first $9,275, but at a rate of 15% for the *next* $28,374 of income. The tax rate jumps again to 25% on income amounts over $37,651 but less than $91,150. This type of tax structure is also called a *progressive tax*, because it keeps increasing with higher income.

Since some part of your income is taxable at one tax rate, and other parts at other tax rates, your overall, combined tax percentage is going to fall somewhere between your highest and lowest marginal tax rates. This is called your **effective tax rate**. Let's take look at a quick example.

John Doe will have $20,000 in taxable income for 2016, and he is single. The first $9,275 of his income is taxed at 10%, as mentioned above, for a tax of $927.50 on that first chunk. The rest of his income is taxed at 15%. The remainder comes to $10,725 ($20k - $9,275). That $10,725 is taxed at 15%, which comes to $1,608.75. Adding the two taxes together equals $2,536.25 in total tax. His tax divided by his taxable income equals 0.1268, or 12.68%. This percentage is John Doe's effective tax rate.

Congress changes the tax rates or the income threshold for each marginal tax rate on an annual basis. It is a large part of the annual political wrangling that goes on in Washington, D.C. between the political parties and different branches of government.

Other Taxes

Besides income taxes, there are other taxes that can be added on to your tax bill on a personal income tax return. The most common example is self-employment tax, which is the equivalent of the Social Security and Medicare taxes that an employer would withhold from your paycheck if you weren't self-employed.

Other taxes that can be added onto your Form 1040 include penalties for early withdrawal of money from retirement accounts, taxes you owe for having household help (such as a maid or nanny), and repayment of certain tax credits, such as the first time home buyer credit from previous years.

Your income tax plus these other taxes are added together to arrive at your total tax.

Tax Credits

Tax credits are important because they have a profound impact on your actual tax bill. Credits don't reduce your taxable income, but rather reduce your tax itself on a dollar for dollar basis. The tax, as calculated above from your taxable income, is some number, which is then reduced $1 for every $1 in tax credits that you are eligible for.

Tax credits are another tool of the political hornet's nest in Congress. Some tax credits are considered "sacred cows" of the system, and much heated debate erupts when a politician suggests changing or eliminating one of them. Other tax credits, such as the home energy efficiency tax credit, are the end result of years of lobbying efforts by special interest groups. Whether you agree or disagree with the political element behind a particular tax credit, the bottom line is that such credits lower your tax bill, and therefore benefit you financially if you are eligible for them.

There are two distinct types of tax credits: **Refundable and non-refundable.** Most tax credits are non-refundable, meaning that if the sum of these tax credits reduces your tax amount to LESS than zero, you do NOT get the difference back as a refund. Refundable credits, on the other hand, can reduce your tax amount to a negative number and the government will send you a check for the difference as a refund.

The single biggest refundable credit is the **Earned Income Credit**. This tax credit is the one responsible for giving several thousand dollar refunds to low income individuals that never actually pay a dime in tax. It is one of the "sacred cows" mentioned above to politicians, and is a very controversial tax credit, because it essentially serves as a wealth redistribution mechanism, literally taking money in the form of taxes to people that have higher incomes and giving it to lower income individuals that pay nothing into the system. The Earned Income Credit (EIC) can be as little as a few dollars for somebody with no children, to as much as several thousand dollars for somebody with multiple children and an AGI of less than $20,000. Again, regardless of your political stance on the issue, if you are eligible for this large tax credit, CLAIM IT!

Other tax credits, such as the Child Tax Credit (non-refundable) and the Additional Child Tax Credit (refundable), are directly related to how many eligible children you have. There is also a tax credit for childcare expenses you pay so you can work. If you sent young children to a daycare or had a babysitter or nanny, you may be eligible for this credit.

Other common tax credits we haven't mentioned already include:

- education credits for paying tuition and other fees (non-refundable and refundable)
- credit for income tax paid to a foreign government (non-refundable)
- retirement savings contribution credit (non-refundable)
- Federal fuel tax credit (refundable)
- credits for doing things to stimulate the economy (refundable)
- specially created economic stimulus credits, such as the (once upon a time) Making Work Pay credit (refundable)

All of these credits have special rules for eligibility. Again, if you even THINK you may be eligible for one, look into, as every dollar counts. These credits are added up and then subtracted from your total tax, and may be enough to turn a tax bill into a refund.

Refund or Amount You Owe

Everything we've discussed to this point on a tax return boils down to one line: The amount you owe or the amount of your refund. By now, the math should make sense: Your total tax minus your tax credits and minus any payments you made throughout the year (such as income tax withholding from your paycheck or estimated tax payments if you're self-employed) equals some number. If that number is positive, you owe money. If it's negative, you get a refund.

Making sure you claim every adjustment, deduction, exemption, tax credit, and tax payment that you are eligible for is just as important as making sure you claim all your income. The difference, however, is that the IRS simply doesn't care if you don't claim all the deductions and credits you're allowed to – they only care that you claim all your income that you're supposed to.

YOU need to be the person that cares most about claiming everything that helps you, and you should make sure that your tax preparer, if you use one, also cares deeply about making sure you claim every tax benefit that you can.

Remember, if you owe the IRS money, your penalties and interest are calculated as a direct percentage of what you owe. By claiming every tax benefit you can under the law, you're not just minimizing your tax bill, you're also minimizing the penalties and interest that you have to pay.

The end result of missing a few hundred dollars in student loan interest deduction, for example, can actually end up being substantially more than that in extra tax, penalties, and interest.

<u>Bottom line: Don't be shy, claim EVERY tax benefit you're legally entitled to!</u>

Tax Resolution Resource

For additional, up to date tips for *minimizing your tax bill* and *maximizing refunds* on your tax returns, please visit:

http://CPAofAtlanta.com

CHAPTER 5

FOUR HEAVY-DUTY, TAX-CUTTING, MONEY-SAVING SECRETS THE IRS DOESN'T WANT YOU TO KNOW

Now that we've covered the anatomy of a tax return and how your tax bill is generated, let's look at four specific strategies for chopping that bill down even further.

Over the course of my career, I've had the pleasure of meeting taxpayers from every walk of life, and from every corner of the country. Many I've met individually and some I've been privileged to visit with or speak to in a group or conference setting.

Funny thing is — of the thousands of questions I've been asked over these many years — the huge majority of them have been centered in five specific areas. There goes another example of the 80/20 rule, a.k.a. the Pareto Principle, in action.

The 80/20 rule is the one that basically says that 80 percent of the cars travel on 20 percent of the roads. And conversely, that 80 percent of the crimes are committed by 20 percent of the people. As I understand it, Pareto was not only an economist but also an avid gardener and botanist. He noticed that 80 percent of his peas came from only 20 percent of his plants.

So, what are the five big questions or topics that we get from 80 percent of more of the people we talk to?

1) What if I owe the IRS? (as in, "What are my options if I owe the IRS?")

2) What if I get audited? (again, as in "What are my options if I get audited?)

3) What can I deduct?

4) What records do I need to keep, and what if my records have been lost, stolen, destroyed by a disgruntled spouse or significant other, or they just plain don't exist?

5) What entity should I use for my business?

While I haven't kept a running list, I'm pretty sure that Questions 1 and 2 are in a dead heat for being the most frequently asked questions in the history of the US income tax.

Obviously, the lion's share of this book discusses Question 1, along with discussing some of the options. We've even included some Case Studies from real clients, or what some may call "True Confessions".

All five of these question areas are literally "dollars and cents", money-in-your-wallet kind of questions. And for that very reason, they are topics that the IRS would prefer to keep hush-hush if at all possible.

Think of it this way: The IRS is the biggest and most feared collection agency on the planet. And if you were a collection agent for any collection agency in the world, how do you suppose your work would be evaluated?

So let's dive right in and address Question 2:

What are my options if:

- I'm getting audited right now?

- I've received a letter telling me I'm going to get audited, or,

- I've already been audited, and I just got a Nasty-gram telling me I owe them $34,000 for the past three years?

First, the bad news: There are some bad auditors out there. But there are also bad doctors and lawyers, so what else is new?

I could easily fill two whole books with strategies for dealing with the IRS in the event that you get that dreaded letter from them. So how about a piece of decent news to offset the above bad news?

Would you like to know what the average audit rate is throughout the country for returns with an income of, let's say, $25,000? Wanna go higher? Okay, how about $200,000? We can go there, too.

The most recent year for which the IRS has published data for audit statistics is for the federal fiscal year ending September 30, 2014.

According to the IRS' own statistics, the nationwide average audit rate for taxpayers, not including a business schedule (such as C, E, or F) was 0.9 percent. **That's less that one out of every hundred returns!**

Even individuals with incomes between $200,000 and $1 million had only a 2.2 percent chance of facing Uncle Sam at the audit desk.

If you have business income, the stats get really interesting:

Entity	Income	Audit Rate
Schedule C	$25,000-$100,000	1.9%
Schedule C	$100,000 or more	2.3%
C Corporations	Assets <$10 million	1.0%
C Corporations	Assets $1 to $5 million	1.2%
C Corporations	Assets $5 to $10 million	1.9%
S Corps & Partnerships	Assets < $10 million	0.4%

So the upshot of these statistics is three-fold:

1) Worst case scenario, you are generally talking about a pretty slim chance of having your number called. So for now, take a breath and step away from the ledge. <u>It probably ain't gonna happen.</u>

2) As you can plainly see from our chart above, the choice of entity makes a <u>huge</u> difference if you have a business of any kind.

    Based upon the above stats, *you can cut your chances of an audit in half or more simply by incorporating your business.*

    This is not me telling you this—these are the IRS' own numbers!

3) As you might imagine, there are definite issues within a specific return that give it more "audit points", e.g., a greater likelihood of being chosen for an audit. Currently, for example, claiming an Earned Income Credit literally doubles your likelihood of an examination, simply because this credit tends to be very abused and lends itself to fraud, misstatement, and even identity theft.

    The IRS does tend to look much more at the filing history for each taxpayer rather than look at a single return by itself. For example, if you take a charitable contributions deduction equal to 8 percent of you 2015 income, the IRS may take a look at two or three prior-year returns to see if you took similar deductions in those years.

But let's try to circle the runway and begin our final approach towards Tax Secret Number 1:

(Surprised you, didn't I? You thought the secret here was the super-low audit rates by the IRS, didn't ya'?)

Let's say your examination has taken place, and that our "friend" the IRS auditor has proposed changes that would result in you owing another $10,000 to the world's largest collection agency.

Where do you go from here?

Sadly, most taxpayers, and *even many attorneys and CPAs* would just say, "Fine, show me where to sign."

WRONG!

Tax Secret #1 is three simple words:

"IRS Appeals Division"

The IRS Appeals Division has the specific responsibility of settling un-agreed audit cases and other disputed claims. Would you care to know your chances of success there?

Are you sitting down?

The IRS' own statistics show that <u>more than 80 percent of all taxpayers that file appeals get their tax bills reduced</u>. That's 80 PERCENT!

Not impressed yet? Well catch this then:

The AVERAGE adjustment is 40 percent!

And in the worst case, even if you lose your appeal, you've succeeded in putting off the tax bill for anywhere from three to six months.

Worried about hiring an expensive tax attorney? Gotcha covered there, too. If your tax bill is less than $50,000, your case will be heard in an informal setting where you can present your own case before a judge, much like a Small Claims Court setting, and it only costs $60 to file that Tax Court petition, plus you don't have to pay the tax ahead of time!

Note: I would still advise you to seek competent legal eagle counsel, even in a "smaller" case.

If the proposed adjustment in your case is a few hundred dollars or less, I would likely advise paying it even if you disagree. Any Tax Court practitioner worth his or her salt will charge that or more just to review your case.

For any proposed amount of more than a few thousand, I strongly recommend talking with a qualified attorney or CPA, well-versed not only in IRS audits, but specifically in dealing with the Appeals Office and Tax Court.

Don't assume that your tax professional, if you have one, is experienced in dealing with either the Examination Division or the Appeals Office and Tax Court. ASK! Even though we do a fair amount of Appeals work in our office, I wouldn't hesitate to get a second opinion from a trusted colleague if we have an especially sticky issue.

Mega-Uber Tax Secret #2:

"What if I don't have good records?"

"Wha-huh?!", you ask. How can you not have records? In a perfect world, we would all have records for every expense we deduct on our tax returns. That's certainly the way that our friends at IRS audit would have it.

If you come face to face with them in an audit, they may even tell you, "No receipt, no deduction!" And they'll stand firm on their decision, not knowing that you now know about Tax Secrets #1 and 2 from *What to Do When the IRS Comes Calling!*

Over the past 20 years or more, we have run across literally hundreds of situations where a taxpayer's financial records had been lost, stolen, or destroyed in a variety of ways.

Some of the stories we have encountered were a bit on the humorous side, and some, well, not so much.

We've had truck drivers and construction contractors return home to be encountered by a disgruntled spouse or significant other in the front yard, just in time to see their tax records literally go up in smoke inside a 55-gallon drum... Along with their favorite acoustic guitar.

Not so humorous was the horrific story after-story that we heard a little over ten years ago in August 2005 when Hurricane Katrina ravaged and flooded thousands of homes and businesses in New Orleans.

Businesses of every kind were wiped out and literally swept away.

By this time, we already had a measure of expertise in records re-construction and estimation of expenses in situations such as this when there is little or no information to start from.

Katrina was our baptism by fire.

We helped as many as we could, and for those that we couldn't, we at least tried to educate them on how to start towards reconstructing and estimating their income and expenses.

When I get to speak to groups around the country, people are often surprised to learn that we use some of the IRS's very own secret methods for re-constructing records and estimating expenses.

Ever hear of an entertainer and songwriter named George M. Cohan?

He's the guy that wrote *Yankee Doodle Dandy* and *You're a Grand Old Flag*.

It seems that Mr. Cohan's income tax returns were audited in the 1940's for a year during which he had travelled with his show for more than 30 weeks during the year.

Unfortunately, Mr. Cohan had not maintained records to back up the expenses he claimed on his tax return. So the IRS examiner disallowed most of his business expenses out of hand.

Fortunately, the story doesn't end there.

He appealed the IRS' disallowance, and eventually the U.S. Tax Court found in his favor.

Thus, his estimated expenses were all allowed and the *Cohan Rule* was born, and has held up ever since then. We have cited it in numerous cases where original records are found to be lacking or even non-existent.

What does this mean for business owners everywhere? It means that if you can reasonably estimate valid expenses for which you have no original records, it is acceptable for you to claim a deduction.

The Cohan Rule came in very handy for the thousands of professional drivers, construction contractors, doctors, lawyers, and other business professionals from the New Orleans area that were left with no records after Hurricane Katrina wreaked havoc on that area.

Separate from the Cohan Rule, you may have had a situation where you actually had good records for, say, three or more consecutive months of the year. The IRS will often allow you to estimate or reconstruct your expenses for the periods for which you don't have records, if your income was relatively steady throughout the year.

Both of these remedies can make a huge difference when the auditor has initially said "no receipts, no deduction". They will likely need to be brought up on Appeal. But they can save you from writing a five-figure check to your least favorite government agency.

Even if you handle your own IRS audit, be sure to seek out a tax firm that specializes in dealing with tax audits also in the IRS Appeal process.

Mega-Uber, Heavy Duty Tax Secret #3:

"What business entity is best for lowering my tax bill?"

Business owners of every kind can literally save themselves thousands <u>every year</u> by getting this one question right.

Until a few years ago, there were three primary forms of operating a business:

- Sole proprietorship

- Partnership

- Corporation (either as a "regular" corporation, or as a "Sub-S" corporation)

In 1977, a new type of entity was created called a limited liability company, or LLC for short. There are still many misconceptions regarding the LLC structure, even among tax and accounting professionals.

I'm going to try and give you a basic idea of where the LLC fits in with the other forms of doing business.

Just as with a corporation, an LLC must be established, or *organized*, through the Secretary of State office in the state where your business will be located.

Thus, if you choose the LLC form of business, it has become your legal form of doing business in your state of organization. One of the beautiful things about the LLC form of business, however, is that you get to <u>choose</u> how you want to be treated for tax purposes by the IRS.

And those options, again, include:

- Sole proprietorship
- Partnership (which requires two or more owners)
- Regular corporation
- S corporations

For tax purposes, if you set up an LLC but choose to have it taxed as a sole proprietorship, then you have gained no advantage whatsoever over the tax man.

In a sole proprietorship, your net income — what's left after business deductions — is subject to both Federal Income Tax, and also Self-Employment Tax, which is the equivalent of Social Security Tax.

The default tax entity, *if you do not make your own election*, is to be taxed as a sole proprietorship.

Rather than go through a dusty, dreary discussion of each form of business, I believe we can address 90 percent of the entity issues with these two statements:

1) Rarely, if ever, should you consider doing business as a partnership.

   In most cases for both tax and legal purposes, the partnership form of business is even worse than simply operating as a sole proprietorship. Why?

   With a partnership, the entire net income of the partnership is taxable to the partners for both Federal Income Tax and also Self-Employment Tax purposes... Even if you didn't take it out as compensation!

   Additionally, any other partner can legally bind and commit you and any other partners for purchases they made-- even without your authorization.

   Granted, there are specific and limited circumstances in which a partnership form of business is beneficial. For example, a family limited partnership may be the best entity if the primary purpose of the entity is to hold and own equipment, such as a fleet of trucks or other heavy machinery.

2) In most cases that we see, the most advantageous tax form of business is to organize an LLC, and make the election to have it taxed as a subchapter S corporation.

   What is it that makes a Sub-S corporation so great?

   With a Sub-S corporation, you get to decide, within reason, how much of your income you want to be subject to Self-Employment Tax (Social Security Tax).

   You are probably thinking—what's the big deal, that's just a few measly bucks? To give you an idea of the difference it can make, let's go through a very real life example:

   Let's say that you have been operating as a sole proprietorship for a few years and you have fairly consistently been netting say, $50,000. Your Self-Employment Tax alone, on that $50,000 net income will be 12.9 percent, or $6,450.

Let's say you want to be ultra-conservative, and that you elect to have just half of your net income be subject to Self-employment tax. Taking half of the $6,450, we get the result of $3,225. Thus, by making this one simple change you have cut your total tax bill by $3,225 in our example. These are savings that you will enjoy year after year to use as you see fit.

Grow your business... or provide for your family... or take that well-deserved vacation you've been dreaming of for years.

Plus, the higher your net income, the more you will save by taking this shrewd but totally legal step.

So now that you've seen a very real example of the very real way that this text secret can save you, let's throw a little more fuel on the fire in favor of the corporation:

Remember earlier in this chapter, when we were talking about the chances of an IRS audit by type of entity?

How about a quick review just in case you were distracted at the moment:

Entity Type	Chances of IRS Audit
Sole Proprietorship	1.9 percent
Regular Corporation	0.9 percent
Sub-S Corporation	0.4 percent

What does the chart tell us? It tells us that, on average, you can cut your chances of the IRS auditing your business by a full 75 percent simply by switching from a sole proprietorship to a Sub-S corporation.

Even if you have every single receipt for every single expense on your return, *that* is some peace of mind that you can sink your teeth into.

Seriously, imagine reducing to nearly nil, the likelihood of being called in for an IRS examination.

So when you add the very real peace of mind to the very real financial savings by using a Sub-S corporation, that is a Heavy-Duty, Tax-Cutting Secret if ever there was one!

My friend Scott Letourneou, a fellow author and colleague, is one of the foremost authorities in the U.S. on entity choice.

I gladly give Scott credit for our expertise in the area of entity choice. He actually makes the same statement in one of his writings that, in most cases, an LLC with the election to be taxed as an S-Corporation will be your best bet.

As with all other tax and legal matters, we strongly recommend that you seek professional counsel for guidance based upon your specific situation.

If you would like to do further research in this area, I gladly recommend Scott Letourneau to you at his website, ScottLetourneau.com.

Super-duper, Heavy-Duty, Tax-Cutting, Money-Saving Strategy #4:

"What can I deduct?"

In our office, one of the services we offer is a low-cost review of prior year tax returns for new clients.

Interestingly, across several of the industries and professions in which we specialize, we typically see that two out of three returns have a sufficient level of overlooked expenses to justify filing amended returns, even after taking our professional fees into account.

If you are a business owner, then hopefully you have discovered that the tax law is skewed very heavily in your favor. And when I say "business owner", I'm really referring to just about anyone that:

1) Is paid on a 1099 rather than a W-2, and,

2) Incurs expenses in the course of producing their income.

The IRS definition of a deductible business expense is one that is *ordinary, reasonable, and necessary* in the conduct of your business. And believe me, that definition leaves a lot of room for very reasonable interpretation.

As I mentioned previously, one of our favorite activities in our firm is to review the prior-year returns of new clients, especially business owners. Even without being aggressive, we find that, on average, about two out of every three returns have sufficient overlooked deductions to justify amending the returns.

POOF—found money!

While we work with a wide variety of clients, we have developed a special level of expertise in a handful of professions and industries:

- Trucking and transportation
- Healthcare, especially nursing related
- Attorneys
- Real estate and finance
- Construction
- Home-based businesses, including direct marketers, coaches, and consultants

While there are specific nuances to the expenses of each of these disciplines, we tend to use a "reasonable person" approach in guiding clients as to the deductibility of an expense. Meaning, would a reasonable person in that profession be likely to consider that an ordinary and necessary cost of doing business?

For example, we have the pleasure of working with truck drivers in just about every state. We are frequently asked if he or she can deduct the care and feeding of a dog for security purposes, to which we usually answer *yes*.

Not so much for a security kitty!

One of the questions we are frequently asked both individually and when speaking to groups throughout the country is, "Is it safe to take a home-office deduction?"

And the answer is, "If you are entitled to take the deduction, it's very safe!"

We have taken a home-office deduction for all of the categories of business owners above with no problems whatsoever, even in the case of a tax audit.

Generally the guidelines for taking a home-office deduction are that the business use for that space be "regular and exclusive".

Numerous colleagues and observers agree that the IRS simply is not placing as much scrutiny on the home-office deduction they did, say, 15 or 20 years ago.

The way we live and work has changed so dramatically that it is not at all uncommon for businesses owners and employees alike to work from a home office.

As a matter of fact, in order to save some taxpayers the aggravation of assembling all the appropriate household expenses that fall into the home office deduction, Congress has passed into law a "safe harbor" home office deduction of $5.00 per square foot of office space that is used.

So let's say that your office is 12 x 12 for a total of 144 square feet. Your home office deduction would be $720.00. Taxpayers are allowed to use this simplified method for office spaces up to 300 square feet and a maximum deduction of $1500.00.

The home office deduction is simply one small example of a valid business expense that taxpayers very commonly overlook.

Another area of overlooked expenses is business mileage. Business owners of every kind tend to under-report their mileage rather than over-report it, so we daily put on our "detective hats" for overlooked business mileage as well as a whole boatload of other expenses that may have been overlooked.

Of all things, my wife, Robin, and I were audited a number of years ago. That particular year, we had gone on a ski trip with friends of ours that also happened to be clients.

When the examiner came to that particular expense, she simply asked, regarding our friends, "Are they either clients or potential clients?" I answered, "Yes ma'am." and she moved on. No qualifying questions at all. She allowed the deduction.

So our final super-duper, tax-cutting secret is this:

Not only are you very likely overlooking perfectly legal and ethical deductions, but you can amend up to three current years of returns to reduce your tax liability and even get a refund of overpaid taxes.

The <u>really</u> big secret is you can amend ANY year for which you still have a balance due in order to reduce your tax bill down to zero. You simply would not be allowed get a refund after three years.

Tax Planning

For additional, up to date tips for minimizing your tax bill and maximizing refunds on your tax returns, get our FREE special report, *"The Top Five Personal Tax-Saving IRS 'Secrets' For Surviving Tough Economic Times"* directly from our website:

www.CPAofAtlanta.com

CHAPTER 6

UNDERSTANDING IRS COLLECTIONS AND THE RESOLUTION PROCESS

The U.S. Internal Revenue Service is the single largest collections agency in the world. In 2015, the IRS spent over $11.9 billion and employed over 82,000 people to collect more than $3.3 trillion in total tax revenue.

Out of that $11.9 billion annual budget, the IRS spent only $2.2 billion processing returns and cashing the checks that Americans sent in voluntarily. Compare that to the $4.9 billion they spent conducting audits and chasing people with tax debts.

Needless to say, this is a bill collector that can have a serious impact on your life, especially given the collections actions they can take that other bill collectors can't.

It is important to understand that the IRS is a slow moving bureaucracy that is highly resistant to change, and is heavily driven by forms and written procedures. This doesn't bode well when it comes to fixing your tax problem quickly, but it does provide a major benefit to working to resolve your tax problem: **Their playbook is public record, and they're required to follow it.**

Here in this chapter, I'm going to provide you an overview of the flow of the IRS collections process and the tax resolution process. Both processes have a very logical, linear flow. In the chapters that follow, we will discuss specific aspects of the tax resolution process, so that you can jump to the chapter and section that is specifically applicable to you, based on where you are in the linear flow of IRS collections.

Collections Starts with a Tax Deficiency

The IRS doesn't start collections activity against you simply because you file a tax return with a balance due and don't pay it. In fact, the collections process really doesn't even start when the tax assessment is made.

In all reality, the IRS collections process begins with a letter called the Statutory Notice of Deficiency (SNOD). Within the industry, we also refer to this as the "21 day letter". This letter is kicked out by a computer automatically when your "number comes up". This can actually be substantially after your tax return was filed. For individuals that file their tax return on time (by April 15th), it's not uncommon to get the SNOD two to four months after the end of tax season. For business that are behind on payroll taxes, I've seen cases where it take an entire year before the IRS kicks out the SNOD. This delay has been one of the primary things reported by the Taxpayer Advocate to Congress as a major problem within the IRS.

The SNOD is referred to as the 21-day letter because it gives you 21 days in which to pay the tax before additional penalties and interest will accrue on the tax liability. Nothing "bad" is going to happen to you during this period.

Notice of Federal Tax Lien Filing (Form 668-Y)

If you fail to pay your tax bill during the 21-day period of the SNOD, don't set up a payment plan, and don't contest the validity of the tax bill, then the next automatic step, again performed by a computer, is the filing of a Notice of Federal Tax Lien (NFTL). Under new rules issues in February 2011, the IRS will only file an actual tax lien against you in your total tax debt exceeds $10,000, including any prior years you may owe for.

As discussed earlier, a tax lien attaches to everything you own, including your wages and all your property. In addition, a tax lien is eventually indicated on your credit report, and can impact you in numerous ways, also discussed in the earlier chapter on tax liens.

Notice of Intent to Levy (Form Letter CP-504)

Approximately 30 to 45 days after the filing of an actual tax lien, a computer will again kick out another notice to you. This notice will be titled "Notice of Intent to Levy" and contain a designation in the upper right or lower right corner labeled "CP-504".

When you receive a CP-504, it is important to know one major thing: It has no real teeth, unless you have a state tax refund coming to you (the IRS can seize that). It is a letter required to be sent to you by law, to notify you that, because of the tax lien, the IRS has the authority to take serious collections action against, such as levies. The letter itself doesn't grant any specific rights to you, but when you receive it, it's important to mark it on the calendar, because 30 days after the CP-504, you're going to get something much, much more important.

Final Notice of Intent to Levy (Letter 11 or 1058)

Exactly 30 days after a CP-504 is issued, you're going to get another form letter from the IRS, labeled "Final Notice of Intent to Levy". In the upper right or lower right corner will be "LT 11" or "Letter 1058".

This letter is important for two reasons:

1. It is the first opportunity you have to file an Appeal.
2. Thirty days after this letter, the IRS can actually levy you.

Here's the bottom line thing to understand about the Letter 1058: If you don't file an Appeal of this notice, the IRS *can* initiate levy action 30 days after they send this notice. In other words, you can safely ignore a lien and a CP-504, but <u>you simply can't ignore a Letter 1058</u>.

Does a Letter 1058 mean that the IRS *will* levy you? No, it doesn't, particularly if they don't have the information necessary to issue a levy. For example, if they don't know where you bank and don't know where you work, they can't very well issue a levy. However, if you still work at the same job that you had when you filed the tax return, the IRS knows where you work, because they received a copy of your W-2 from your employer. Also, if you have in the past given the IRS your bank account number and bank routing number in order to have a refund direct deposited, then they know where your bank is.

Whenever you receive a Letter 1058, you should file an Appeal. In order to do this, file Form 12153, *Request for Collection Due Process Appeal*. Further information about filing this appeal, called a "CDP" for short, and is available in the Appeals chapter, later in this book. Normally, in my practice I will file a CDP appeal about 20 days into the 30 day window for doing so, in order to give my client as much time as possible to get their finances in order.

The Cycle Repeats

The cycle of SNOD → NFTL → CP-504 → Letter 1058 repeats itself any time you incur a new tax liability. For individual taxpayers, that means this cycle could repeat itself once per year. For a business dealing with employment taxes, this cycle could basically never end, since payroll tax returns are filed quarterly, and this cycle takes about 4 months to complete.

Revenue Officer Assignment

Your first time through this cycle, your case will exist within a division of the IRS called the Automated Collection System (ACS). ACS personnel are located at several of the largest IRS service centers, including Ogden, UT, Cincinnati, OH, and Philadelphia, PA. The majority of letters you receive from the IRS will be from one of these service centers.

Unless your collections case has special circumstances associated with it, you will usually stay assigned to ACS even if you accumulate two or three years' worth of tax debt as an individual, or 3 or 4 quarters of payroll tax liability for a business. After reaching this threshold, your case will likely be assigned to a Revenue Officer. Revenue Officers (RO) are field agents that live and work in local community all over the United States. There are currently over 14,000 of these personnel working for the IRS.

An interesting thing about the current economic situation is that there are a growing number of taxpayers falling into trouble with the IRS. Because of this, the waiting line for assignment to an RO is many areas of the country is growing longer and longer. Certain taxpayers are bumped ahead of the line, depending on their circumstances. But for most taxpayers, they are waiting longer and longer, which gives them more and more time to get their finances in order and hopefully be able to work out something once they *do* get assigned to a field agent.

I've mentioned several times that there are certain circumstances that will get you assigned to a Revenue Officer much faster. Some of those circumstances include:

- your total tax debt is particularly large
- your tax liability for a particular year is quite large
- you've accumulated personal tax debt for three or more years
- you have more than 4 quarters of payroll tax liability and continue to accrue more
- you owe taxes and are not actively making Federal Tax Deposits (payroll taxes) or Estimated Tax Payments (if you're self-employed)

When you are assigned to a Revenue Officer, the course of your tax case takes a sudden shift. Having an experienced, trained human being looking at your tax case, and passing judgment on you based on what's in a file and thereby determining how they are going to handle your tax case, means a lot.

The Tax Resolution Process

Whether your case is still assigned to ACS, or if it's been assigned to a Revenue Officer, there is a fairly standard, step-by-step process by which your tax case gets resolved. Since the IRS has their own procedures that employees have to follow, you can always know what the next action from the IRS Collections division is going to be.

In general, these are the steps that you will need to follow to make progress towards a successful and permanent tax resolution:

1. Contact ACS or your Revenue Officer and negotiate a time period of 30 to 120 days in order to get your affairs in order for resolving your tax situation.

2. File appeals on any items which you are eligible to do so.

3. File all past due tax returns, including replacing SFR's.

4. Complete a Collection Information Statement, including supporting documentation, to determine your current financial condition.

5. Determine the best resolution strategy based on your financial condition.

6. Apply for and negotiate towards the chosen resolution strategy.

7. Go through the Appeals process, if necessary.

8. Apply for a penalty abatement, if necessary.

These are the same big picture steps that I follow myself when working with a client.

CHAPTER 7

GOVERNMENT RUBBER GLOVE: THE IRS FINANCIAL PROBE

The Collection Information Statement is a financial instrument that the IRS uses to gather information to determine your ability to pay. This is a personal or business financial statement that gathers information regarding your assets, income, expenses and various other financial items.

Keep in mind that the IRS has established standards for allowable and necessary monthly living expenses. There are certain expenses that the IRS does not allow you to claim when preparing this statement and analyzing your financial condition. For example, the IRS disallows payments on unsecured debt such as credit cards. The IRS also does not give you credit for tuition, payments, 401K contributions or charitable donations. The national standards and local standards for necessary living expenses as set by the IRS consist of food, housekeeping supplies, apparel, and personal care products and services. It also includes housing, utilities, and transportation expenses which are adjusted based on regional differences.

Taxpayers are not required to provide documentation concerning the amount of expenses categorized as national standards for your corresponding income level. However, you are required to substantiate expenses categorized as local standards or other necessary expenses. Keep in mind that the IRS considers necessary expenses to only be those that provide for the health and welfare of you and your family or that relate to the production of income. These expenses must also be reasonable in amount. Some examples of other necessary expenses that the IRS may allow include child care, dependent care for the elderly and the disabled, other taxes, health care, court-ordered payments such as child support, secured debts such as your car payments, term life insurance, disability insurance, union dues, professional association dues, and accounting and legal fees for IRS representation.

The IRS Collection Information Statement is the primary form from which your eligibility for the various IRS resolution programs is determined. In particular, you will be ***required*** to provide this form to the IRS whenever you are applying for:

- Currently Not Collectible Status
- Offer in Compromise
- Installment Agreement

There are actually three different versions of the Collection Information statement. In conversation, practitioners and the IRS refer to the form as just the "433", but the three versions do serve different purposes:

- Form 433-F: The short version for individual taxpayers and married couples, used by the Automated Collection System (ACS) personnel that you talk to on the phone.

- Form 433-A: The long version for individuals, married couples, and businesses that are sole proprietorships. The 433-A is used by field agents such as Revenue Officers, and also the version you should use when submitting an Offer in Compromise.

- Form 433-B: The business version, used for all purposes when the taxpayer is a business other than a sole proprietorship.

The best way to look at the Form 433 is to think of it as a loan application. If you think of it in those terms, the form suddenly makes a lot more sense. In reality, it actually IS a loan application in many regards, especially if you are applying for an Installment Agreement to make monthly payments on your tax debt.

How to Fill Out Form 433

Each of the three different versions of the form have slightly different sections and questions. However, they are obviously more alike than different, even between the individual versus business versions.

The major difference between the Form 433-A and the Form 433-B is that the Form 433-A asks for information regarding your children and other dependents, and also about your employment information.

Warning! *Providing the IRS with your current employment information gives them the information they need in order to issue wage garnishments!*

The other big difference between the 433-A and B is that the income and expense portion of the Form 433-A for individuals includes a column for the Revenue Officer to fill in "Allowable Expenses". At the end of this chapter, we will go through an in depth explanation of allowable expenses, IRS National Standards, and disallowed expenses.

Note: If you run a business as a sole proprietorship or are self-employed, then you should fill out Form 433-A for your business. Pages 5 and 6 of the Form 433-A contain many of the same sections as the Form 433-B regarding the business operation.

Because of the similarities between the forms, and the fact that, as indicated above, the Form 433-A does actually contain business information sections for self-employed individuals, we're going to go through each section of the IRS Form 433-B, *Collection Information Statement for Businesses*, in order to give you detailed information regarding how to fill out each section.

Section 1 - Business Information: This section is pretty straight forward.

If you don't have information regarding the incorporation date, you can obtain that information from the Articles of Organization or Articles of Incorporation, available from the Secretary of State's office where the company was formed. This date should also be in the upper right corner of each year's business tax return.

For line 3c, frequency of tax deposits, this is specifically for businesses with employees. The vast majority of small businesses are required to deposit payroll taxes on a monthly basis, but some may have a large enough payroll to be required to make semi-weekly payments.

Lines 5 and 6 have to do with online payment processing and credit cards accepted by the business. If the company doesn't sell online, mark "no" for line 4, and leave line 5 blank. If the business accepts credit cards, fill in that information on line 6.

Section 2 – Business Personnel and Contacts: Please realize that whomever is listed as the "Person Responsible for Depositing the Payroll Taxes" may be investigated for the Trust Fund Recovery Penalty.

List the officers and owners of the business. Provide their Social Security numbers, home addresses, phone numbers, and what percentage of the business they own.

Section 3 – Other Financial Information:

This series of questions all require a yes/no answer. Check the appropriate box and provide the necessary explanation and other information for any "yes" answers.

For line 14, unless there is an actual event taking place, such as a major new client that will be paying the business a lot of money, mark this question as "no".

Section 4 – Business Assets & Liabilities:

My clients tend to overestimate the value of their assets. They often think in terms of what they paid for something and what it would cost to replace. However, for this section values indicated shouldn't even be Fair Market Value of the item, but actually should be the "liquidation value". Liquidation value is generally what something would sell for at auction.

The IRS wants assets information for a variety of reasons. For one, it is used in the calculation of an Offer in Compromise offer amount. Second, the IRS is looking for large value assets that you might be able to either sell or borrow money against in order to pay the IRS.

If you are still paying on any loans used to purchase the assets, be sure that information is included on the form.

Keep in mind that the Form 433-B is for a *business* – not yourself personally. Therefore, no personal assets should be listed on this form, only things actually owned by the business.

Specific line items:

#16 Bank Accounts - Indicate the name and address of the financial institution where you bank. Provide routing number (it will be nine digits), your account number and your current balance. **Warning:** Providing the IRS with your bank account information gives them the information they need in order to issues levies against your bank accounts!

#17, 18 Accounts Receivable - An Account Receivable is a customer that you did work for or provided products to, but they haven't paid you yet. Attaching a QuickBooks or similar printout is perfectly acceptable. If your business is a Federal government contractor, keep in mind that the *Federal Levy Program* will intercept any payments on your government contract and route that money to the IRS instead.

#19 Investments – Investments are things that could potentially be liquidated in order to pay the tax liability.

#20 Available Credit – List only lines of credit and credit cards that are in the name of the business, not in the name of an individual only. For credit cards, do not list trade or store cards, but only major credit cards such as Visa, MasterCard, and American Express.

#21 Real Estate: List any real estate owned by the business, how much it's worth, who the lender is, and how much is owed and the monthly payment. Also be sure to list property or commercial space that you rent, and include your lease information.

#22 Vehicles, Leased and Purchased: If it's got wheels and moves, list it here. That includes things like trailers, backhoes, airplanes, etc. For the value, I normally use Kelly Blue Book to find values of vehicles, and will look in trade publications, eBay, and Craigslist to get an idea of values for other types of equipment. If there is a loan or lease against the vehicle, include the lender, loan balance, and monthly payment.

#23 Business Equipment: These are large business assets that are bolted down. Again, be sure to provide loan information if any equipment is leased or financed.

#24 Business Liabilities: List here other loans not mentioned elsewhere on the 433-B. These will often be bank loans, Small Business Administration loans, notes, judgments, and other debts that aren't securing equipment or real estate.

Section 5 – Monthly Income and Expenses:

This section is also very important. The difference between the expenses and income is the monthly profit of the business. This amount is used in Offer in Compromise calculations, determines eligibility for Currently Not Collectible status, and determines your monthly payment under an Installment Agreement.

In essence, this section is nothing but a shortened Profit and Loss statement. It is imperative that no expenses are omitted, so attach a Profit and Loss statement itself if necessary, or a listing of "Other" expenses for line #46.

Signature Block

Be sure to sign as a company officer by indicating your position within the company. Keep in mind also that you are signing this form under penalty of perjury.

Attachments Required

When representing a client, the single biggest impediment to obtaining a resolution of their tax liability with the IRS is obtaining all the supporting documentation that we need in order to properly work on their case. The vast majority of the time, I am inevitably submitted a Form 433-B for a client with large sections of the form blank and without significant supporting documentation.

The form itself, at the bottom, has a thorough list of what the IRS expects to see. Keep in mind that they expect copies of 3 months' worth of any particular item, such as bills and statements.

Fortunately, the vast majority of the time a Revenue Officer doesn't complain about the lack of full supporting documentation. At an absolute minimum, just about every IRS Revenue Officer is going to absolutely insist upon receiving the following:

1. Copies of business bank statements for the last 3 months.

2. A Profit and Loss statement covering at least the last 3 months, but usually a Year To Date Profit and Loss.

3. At least one copy of a statement for each and every loan included on the 433-B.

In most cases, providing this minimum list of documentation will appease most Revenue Officers and Appeals Officers. If you are submitting the Form 433-B in support of an Offer in Compromise application and only submit this minimum list of supporting documentation, then you can expect a letter from the Offer in Compromise Process Examiner requesting all the information that you didn't include.

IRS National Standards and Allowable Expenses

As mentioned earlier, the income and expense section of the Collection Information Statement for individuals is quite a bit different than it is for businesses. Businesses are allowed to claim any reasonable business expense, and the Revenue Officer assigned to the case is allowed to (and often does) question any expenses that look fishy.

For individuals, though, the IRS sets very specific limits on what a household can claim as an expense, and also explicitly prohibits claiming certain expenses for collection purposes, *including expenses that are deductible or create tax credits on a tax return.* Many taxpayers are confused by this fact, and it is just one of the numerous inconsistencies across the tax code.

It should also be noted that the IRS National Standards are used by many other Federal agencies for various other purposes. The most common other purpose is that these expense guidelines are utilized by the bankruptcy courts for determining whether a bankruptcy filer ("petitioner") should be allowed to file for Chapter 7 bankruptcy or not (Chapter 7 is a liquidation of your assets and a "flushing" of your debts, whereas Chapter 13 is to set up a payment plan for several years to pay back your creditors).

Many people are shocked at how low some of the numbers are when they look at the National Standards. There are other people that are shocked, however, at how big some of the numbers are. Keep in mind that the IRS National Standards reflect the government's calculation regarding a precisely middle class existence. For example, the allowable housing expense will vary geographically, because housing is cheaper in some parts of the United States, and much, much more expensive in other parts. However, the allowable expense for any area represents the <u>median</u> housing cost for that geographical area.

National Standards for Transportation

The IRS sets national standards for transportation, including public transit, vehicle ownership costs, and vehicle operating costs.

Public transit allowable expense: $182 per month

Vehicle ownership cost, one car: $496 per month

Vehicle ownership cost, two cars: $992 per month

The IRS also sets operating allowances for operating costs, which varies by geographical region. This allowance ranges from a low of $212 per vehicle to a max of $346 per vehicle, per month, depending upon where you live.

National Standards for Food, Clothing, etc.

The IRS sets national standards for allowable expenses for the following typical household items:

- food, including eating in and dining out
- household supplies, such as cleaning, garden, postage, etc.
- clothing, shoes, dry cleaning, tailoring, etc.
- personal care and hygiene products and services
- "miscellaneous" household expenses

The allowable expense for these categories can be claimed without documenting what you actually spend. If you spend more than this amount, then the IRS is going to insist that you document the excess spending.

The IRS national standards for the above items are based on how many people are in your household. For example, they might look like this:

One person: $534 per month

Two people: $985 per month

Three people: $1,171 per month

Four people: $1,377 per month

For each additional person, add $262 per month

Health Care Costs

Taxpayers are also allowed to claim the actual cost of their health insurance premiums, plus $60 per month for each person in the household that is under 65 years of age, and $144 per person that is older than 65. Again, these expenses can be claimed regardless of what you actually spend. If it's more, then you will need to document what you spend.

Housing and Utilities

For most families, the money they spend on putting a roof over their head and keeping the lights on represents not only the single largest household expense, but also the one that fluctuates the most across the country.

The allowance for housing and utilities costs is also based on the number of people in the household. The range of allowable expense is quite large. For example, the range goes from a low of $671 per month for a single person in McDowell County, West Virginia, to a high of $4,041 per month for a family of five or larger in Marin County, California.

Unlike most of the other standardized expenses, you are only allowed to claim the *lesser* of the allowable expense or what you actually spend.

Summary

It is important to claim every allowable expense on your Form 433. Doing so will ultimately minimize the amount you end up paying the IRS on your back tax liabilities.

Tax Resolution Resource

For up to date tables of IRS Collections Standards and allowable expenses for your local area, go to:

https://www.irs.gov/businesses/small-businesses-self-employed/collection-financial-standards

…or just call me at (770) 984-8008 and we can walk through it with you. ☺

CHAPTER 8

SNATCHING VICTORY FROM THE JAWS OF DEFEAT

We totally love getting to share the good news of a favorable result in an IRS case. But some cases allow us the privilege of confirming that we are doing what we were meant to do.

Such was this case, a fairly recent one.

This involved a trucking company here in the Atlanta area that owed over a million dollars to the IRS in taxes, penalties, and interest.

This had been a fairly profitable company, running about 20 trucks and grossing about $2.5 million a year for a few years. They were happy just to have survived the recession, but their balance owed to the IRS for unpaid payroll taxes was more than this family-owned business could withstand.

This was, and still is, a dear, dear family, and I will cherish the friendship we have developed.

We put our very best efforts into every IRS case that we agree to take. But we knew early on that this family had already gone to the mat for years on end to take care of their employees, drivers, and customers.

So we wanted to show them the same courtesy.

The company had gotten extremely under water with the IRS, to the point where they owed literally a million dollars to Uncle Sam, including penalties and interest.

With this huge balance, it was no surprise that their case had already been assigned to a Revenue Officer.

In the IRS system, the Revenue Officer has very far-reaching authority and power. But this can be very much a double-edged sword, as you will see shortly.

In a separate case about two years ago, we took a case representing a trucking company owner and his wife in Louisiana that owed over $100,000 in taxes. The Revenue Officer in that case was entirely overbearing, and was doing everything possible to put our client out of business.

Fortunately, we were able to get the case transferred away from the "Wicked Witch of the West", along with a very pleasant settlement to boot!

Getting back to this case, as it turns out we had had other cases with this Revenue Officer. We recalled that he placed a premium on regular communication with his office.

So we make it a rule to go overboard in calling or faxing him almost every time we sneezed.

But part of what we began communicating was the severe health issues that the husband and wife owners were facing, along with their son, who had previously been one of the company's back-up drivers.

Early on in this case, I asked the owner's wife what amount of monthly payment to the IRS would be manageable for her, at least for the moment, as nothing more than a gesture of good faith. She could live with $1,500 a month.

Now, mind you, settling a delinquent tax balance with the IRS is definitely not the kind of thing where they ask you, "What would you like to pay each month?"

Especially not with a balance of over a million dollars, and most definitely not when the balance is for delinquent payroll taxes.

The IRS takes an extremely dim view of unpaid payroll taxes.

If a business already owes, say, $150,000 or more in payroll taxes, and is <u>still</u> not paying—or not able to pay—the current payroll taxes, thus the balance is continuing to grow, this practice is known within the IRS as *pyramiding*.

The IRS will shut down a business faster than you can say, "Danger, Will Robinson!" for continuing this practice.

Withheld payroll taxes are, in effect, the IRS' money, because all of the employees from whom it was withheld will be receiving a W-2 showing the amount of Federal Withholding, along with, of course, Social Security and Medicare.

So our very first order of business was to get them current for at least a couple of quarters, even if they could pay nothing towards the arrearage of a million dollars and some change.

We created and discussed with the trucking company owners a game plan for getting into compliance for two consecutive quarters, a six month period.

And again, going back to our knowledge of this particular Revenue Officer, we even called him and told him our plan and told him we would even send him something in writing that would lay out our proposed steps in numerical order.

I even mentioned to him that we would be helping the company with a plan towards their quarterly payroll, which, in time, would help them reduce the quarterly payroll taxes that they had to pay in. In this case, that simply meant that we would help our trucking client to take the appropriate steps towards converting several drivers from being company drivers to owner-operators, compensated on a 1099 rather than a W-2.

So over the next several months, we began giving him updates as to the family's health issues as well as the effect on the economy of their business.

All while making absolutely certain that the company kept current on their payroll taxes for current quarters.

Over this period of time, we showed a picture that if the company stayed current with their taxes and also paid the current medical bills they would only have about $250 per month left over to go towards that million dollar tax debt.

Eventually, I sent updated financial information to the Revenue Officer that showed the family was "in the red" on an average monthly basis. Even with that information, I requested an Installment Agreement of $150 per month.

We waited…and waited…and waited some more.

After getting no response for almost three weeks, we used a special process for practitioners where we are able to see online what is going on with the business or individual taxpayer account.

The online transcript showed that the revenue officer had declared our clients' IRS account as "Currently Not Collectible". <u>This means that the Service will not require payments towards the prior balance for as much as three years.</u>

Eventually, the Revenue Officer informed us of this action and said he would simply renew the "Not Collectible" status whenever it came up for review <u>as long as the business owners stayed current</u>.

Thus, their million dollar tax debt will eventually just expire—in about six years in this particular case. In other words, the liability will "fall off" entirely.

One of our most successful cases ever, and it couldn't have come at a better time for a very deserving family.

CHAPTER 9

TAX DEBT RESOLUTION OPTIONS

When you're trying to resolve tax matters with the IRS, you have a number of different options. Depending on your financial circumstances and the amount of your IRS back tax liability and other issues, you have several options available to you. In this chapter we will give you a brief overview of some of these options.

A Brief Word on Offers in Compromise

The Offer in Compromise is probably the most commonly known tax resolution strategy. This is what you hear about in TV commercials and radio ads, particularly when they talk about settling your tax debt for "pennies on the dollar" (a phrase which the IRS has technically banned advertisers from using). However, it is important to keep in mind that not everybody even qualifies for an Offer in Compromise, not to mention that this is only one of the many options that might be available to you.

Each option must be explored in relation to the specific facts and circumstances surrounding your tax problem and then the best option can be selected and implemented. In some instances it may be necessary to employ two or more options to settle your tax obligations.

Keep in mind that the ultimate goal is to solve your tax problem permanently and for the lowest amount allowed by law.

Option 1 – Full pay the tax owed

While seldom a popular option, sometimes you may have the ability to pay the tax outright or borrow against an existing asset, such as a cash out refinance of the equity in your home. Surprisingly, in this situation this option is usually the least costly of viable options available to you. The reason for this is simple. One, your equity and assets will usually disqualify you from benefiting from options which grant debt forgiveness. Second, until the tax debt is paid in its entirety it will continue to accrue penalties and interest. Generally, the combined penalty and interest rates that the IRS charges you are going to be significantly more than the interest rate you will pay from borrowing the money elsewhere.

Option 2 – Filing unfiled tax returns and replacing Substitute for Returns

When resolving a tax problem it is relatively common to have unfiled back tax returns. There are three reasons why it is necessary to file these returns and become current with your filing obligations.

1. Failure to file tax returns may be construed as a criminal act by the IRS and can be punishable by one year in jail for each year not filed. Filing unfiled tax returns brings you "current."

2. Filing unfiled returns to replace Substitute for Returns may lower your tax liability and the associated interest in penalties because the interest and penalties is calculated from the tax debt amount. A "Substitute for Return" (SFR) is when the IRS uses whatever information that they have available to them to prepare a tax return on your behalf. Now, most of the time this tax return that they prepare is not going to take into account your expenses, your credits, and any allowable deductions. In other words, an SFR prepared by the IRS

based just on the copy of your W-2 that an employer filed with the IRS is <u>not</u> going to be in your favor.

3. A settlement cannot be negotiated with the IRS until you become completely current with all filing obligations.

Option 3 – Dispute the tax on technical grounds

If there is a technical basis to dispute the amount of tax owed, there are a number of paths to consider, such as filing an amended return if the statute of limitations to file has not expired or filing an Offer in Compromise under Doubt as to Liability criteria. If you are currently in an audit situation and the math on the audit is simply not right then you can contest the tax on these technical grounds by fighting for the correct calculations.

Option 4 – Currently Not Collectible Status

If you do not have positive cash flow above the level necessary to pay your minimum living expenses or you lack sufficient equity in assets to liquidate and pay the tax, you may qualify for Currently Not Collectible status (CNC). This is most commonly seen when you are either unemployed or underemployed. In this situation, the IRS places a temporary hold on the collection of the tax owed until your financial situation improves. If over a longer period of time your situation does not improve, you may eventually become a viable Offer in Compromise candidate.

Option 5 – Installment Agreements

In the vast majority of cases, the IRS will accept some type of payment arrangement for past due taxes. In order to qualify for a payment plan, you must meet set criteria, which includes the following, among other things:

- You must file all past due returns.
- You must disclose all assets that you own.
- You must provide information regarding your monthly income and monthly expenses.

The difference between your monthly income and allowable expenses is the amount that the IRS will expect to receive from you under the payment plan.

Monthly payments can be expected to continue until the taxes owed are paid in full. However, it is possible to obtain a Partial Payment Installment Agreement (PPIA). A PPIA means that you'll have an Installment Agreement in place until the Statute of Limitations for collection of the tax expires. After the Statute of Limitations expires, the tax literally just goes away, along with all penalties and interest. The date on which the IRS can no longer attempt to collect the tax from you is called the Collection Statute Expiration Date (CSED).

Option 6 – The Offer in Compromise

The IRS Offer in Compromise program allows you to pay the IRS less than the full amount of your tax, penalties, and interest, and pay only a small amount as a full and final settlement. This program also has an option for Doubt as to Liability. In these cases you disagree with the amount of the tax assessment and this gives you a chance to file an Offer in Compromise and have your tax assessment itself reconsidered.

The Offer in Compromise program allows taxpayers to get a fresh start. In this process, all back tax liabilities are settled with the amount of the Offer in Compromise. Once the payment amount of the Offer in Compromise is fully paid off, all Federal tax liens are released. An Offer in Compromise that is based on your inability to pay is decided upon when the IRS looks at your current financial position, your ability to pay (income minus expenses), as well as your equity in assets.

These factors will dictate the amount that can be offered. You can compromise all types of IRS taxes, penalties, and interest in one fell swoop. Even payroll taxes, which are often the most difficult to resolve, can be compromised. If you qualify for the Offer in Compromise program, you may be able to save thousands and thousands of dollars in tax, penalty, and interest.

Option 7 – Penalty Abatements

In most cases penalties make up 10-30% of your total tax obligation. A penalty abatement request can eliminate some or all of the penalties if you have reasonable cause for not paying the tax on time or paying the appropriate amount of tax. Reasonable cause includes the following: prolonged unemployment, business failure, major illness, incorrect accounting advice or bad advice from the IRS. To prevail in a penalty abatement request as in most tax matters, the burden rests with you to be able to adequately document the reasonable cause.

Option 8 – Discharging taxes in bankruptcy

Bankruptcy can discharge federal income tax if certain requirements are met. However, this depends upon both the type of bankruptcy and the type of tax owed. Chapter seven is the chapter of bankruptcy law that provides for the liquidation of non-exempt assets and the discharge of dischargeable debts. Chapters 11 and 13 provide for repayments of debt in whole or in part. To discharge taxes in bankruptcy, a number of criteria must be met:

1. Thirty-six months have lapsed from the tax return due date.

2. Twenty-four months have lapsed from the date the tax was assessed.

3. At least 240 days have passed since the tax was assessed and filing of bankruptcy.

4. All of your tax returns have to have been filed.

Option 9 – Innocent Spouse Relief

It is not uncommon to find yourself in trouble with the IRS because of your spouse or ex-spouses' actions. The IRS realizes that these situations do in fact occur. In order to help you with tax problems which are due to the actions of your spouse, the IRS has developed guidelines for you to qualify as an innocent spouse. If the taxpayer can prove that they meet these guidelines then the innocent taxpayer may not have to pay some or all the taxes caused by their spouse or ex-spouse.

Option 10 – Expiration of the Collection Statute

The IRS only has a limited time during which to collect back taxes from you. This time period starts on the date of the assessment of the tax and runs for 10 years. After the 10 years has lapsed, you no longer owe taxes, penalties or interest on that tax period.

There are of course exceptions to this rule. You may agree in writing to allow the IRS more time to collect the tax. If you file an Offer in Compromise or if you file bankruptcy, these actions can both cause automatic extensions on the 10-year period. In these situations the amount of time for the IRS to collect the tax is extended usually by the amount of time that the action is in place.

So for example, if you file an Offer in Compromise and it takes six full months for the IRS to process your Offer in Compromise and give you a determination then the statute of limitations on collection is extended by another six months.

If the IRS attempts to collect the tax obligation which is expired under the 10-year rule, the taxpayer must inform the IRS in writing that the statute of limitations has expired. Once this notification occurs the tax can be forgiven. So therefore, if you have tax liabilities that the IRS is trying to collect that are more than 10 years old, it is imperative that you calculate the exact Collection Statute Expiration Date or CSED for short and notify the IRS in writing that they are no longer allowed to collect on that tax if the date is passed the CSED.

Tax Resolution Resource

IRS Fresh Start Program

In 2011 the IRS announced a new effort to help struggling taxpayers get a fresh start. **Do you qualify?**

Please contact me via my web site at http://CPAofAtlanta.com for help determining if you may qualify for that program.

CHAPTER 10

TIME: IT'S EITHER ON YOUR SIDE OR THEIR'S
(OK, JUST THEIRS)

Statutes of limitations in regards to tax matters are important for you to understand because the different statutes of limitations give you different rights and responsibilities in regards to the tax matters involved. There are some statutes of limitations that work for you and there are others that can obviously work against you. It is important for you to understand these statutes of limitations when dealing with the Internal Revenue Service so that you aren't chasing the wind or trying to make a case that can't be made.

From the government's perspective, the statute of limitations restricts your rights in many ways, such as the restriction on claiming a refund of tax you overpaid or limiting initial actions to obtain refunds.

Now, a statute of limitations may also restrict what the IRS can do against you. The statute of limitations restricts them from collecting a deficiency in tax after a certain amount of time, and also prevents the IRS from asserting either civil or criminal cases.

Either way you look at it, the statute of limitations issue provides a date of finality after which actions may not be taken by either the IRS or by you which is why it is essential for you to understand them.

Let's first look at the three-year rules. First, the IRS must assess a tax within three years after the date that you file a tax return. This three-year period also applies to penalties. Now, when is a tax return considered filed for the purposes of this rule? A return is treated as being filed on time even if it's received by the IRS after the return's due date.

Timely filing is determined by the postmark stamped on the envelope by the U.S. Postal Service or by a private delivery service. That is why whenever you send a tax return or other important items such as an Installment Agreement proposal or an Offer in Compromise application, or an Appeal, I highly recommend that you always send it by certified mail with return receipt requested.

There does not appear to be a "bright line" test to determine whether a tax return lacking a required form is a valid return. Courts will typically apply the "substantial compliance standard" to the facts of each case. This means that there must be adequate information on the return to calculate the tax liability even if a required form was omitted. The document must also indicate that it is, in fact, a tax return. An honest and reasonable attempt must be made to satisfy the tax law and you must execute the return under penalties of perjury, which is what you're doing whenever you sign the bottom of a tax return. Next time you have a tax return in front of you, take a look at what you're actually signing.

A complete tax return that lacks a specific required form such as a schedule or attachment is still sufficient to begin the statute of limitations running for assessment purposes. So for example, if you file your 1040 personal income tax return but you forget to include a Schedule E. Your income from that Schedule E is on the front page of the Form 1040. The IRS can't say that you didn't file a timely return and therefore they have to start the clock ticking on the statute of limitations for the assessment of the tax as soon as they get it.

There are special statute of limitations rules that you need to be aware of as well. When the IRS produces a Substitute for Return – which is prepared by the IRS when you don't file the tax return – this does not start running the statute of limitations for assessment.

In order to start the clock running on the 3-year assessment statute of limitations, you have to file a tax return yourself. So, if you have been notified by the IRS that they prepared the return on your behalf, it is generally advisable to file an actual, original return as soon as possible.

A six-year statute of limitations, instead of three years, applies to returns that omit a substantial amount of income. "Substantial" means an amount of income which exceeds 25% of the gross income reported on the original tax return. The limitations period is extended to the tax payer's entire tax liability for that year, not just the omitted items.

This applies only to innocent or negligent omissions of gross income. The six-year limitations period does not apply to fraudulent omissions of gross income. If you fraudulently omit reporting income on a tax return, the tax may be assessed at any time.

Here's a bonus tip for you: The burden of proof rests with the IRS in proving that the 25% omission from income did in fact occur. The IRS cannot solely rely on the amount of unreported income asserted in the Notice of Deficiency they mail you, which they're required to send you by law

The Internal Revenue Code states that the IRS can assess tax or bring a suit to collect an unassessed tax at any time regardless of any statute of limitations for some specific situations. Here are those situations:

1. You fail to file the tax return.

2. A false or fraudulent return is filed with the intent to evade the tax.

3. The tax payer attempts to defeat or evade the tax.

4. Once the tax payer files a fraudulent return, the tax payer cannot later start the running of the three-year statute of limitations period by filing an amended return to include the omitted income.

Next, let's talk about statute of limitations on collection of a tax. Once the IRS has assessed the tax within the assessment statute of limitations as discussed above, the IRS then has 10 years in which to collect the tax. There are certain events that can extend the statutory period past the 10-year mark, because they actually "stop the clock". These events include:

- filing bankruptcy

- filing certain appeal requests

- entering into litigation with the IRS

- filing an Offer in Compromise

- filing a request for an Installment Agreement

- requesting a military deferment

- filing an innocent spouse defense

With these actions, the statute of limitations is temporarily suspended while that action is being investigated.

The date of assessment is the date the Assessment Officer signs the Summary Record of Assessment. This information can be verified by obtaining an IRS account transcript called a Record of Account, which you can request from the IRS at any time. If the Summary Record of Assessment was not properly recorded, then the assessment is actually not proper. Some penalties have a different assessment date from that of the original tax. In those cases the penalty has a separate Collection Statute Expiration Date (CSED), which is the date that the 10-year period ends.

The IRS can use administrative or judicial methods to collect delinquent taxes. The IRS generally precedes administratively by levying and seizing assets that you own. If the IRS embarks upon this course of action, the levy must occur within the 10-year statute of limitations period. The IRS can also precede judicially by filing a lawsuit against you within the 10-year limitation period.

During a period of time in which an Installment Agreement request is pending with the IRS, the statute of limitations on collections is suspended for a while. The period is 30 days following a rejection of a proposed Installment Agreement or 30 days following the termination of an Installment Agreement. The statute of limitations on collections is also suspended during an Offer in Compromise investigation. During the time that the IRS is considering your Offer in Compromise, the statute of limitations clock isn't running. It is also not running for the 30 days following the rejection of an Offer in Compromise.

The situation is similar for bankruptcy. A bankruptcy petition prohibits the IRS from assessing or collecting a claim from you which arose prior to the bankruptcy petition being filed. During this period the assessment limitations period – the three- and six-year period as discussed earlier – is suspended, plus a period of 60 days after the discharge of your bankruptcy. The limitation period for collection is suspended during your bankruptcy petition period and for an additional six months after the bankruptcy is discharged.

There are times, which you'll read about later in this book, where an Appeals Officer is involved in your case. The settlement authority of an Appeals Officer is very broad. However, their primary job is to resolve the tax issue expeditiously and to weigh the costs of potential litigation for the IRS. The appeals process is one where professional negotiation skills can really come in handy. Since the appeals process relies so much upon negotiation, a high percentage of cases are resolved here. It is not uncommon for those of us that are professional tax resolution representatives to simply resolve our clients' cases in the appeals process rather than relying on a field Revenue Officer to work with us.

The biggest thing that you need to remember is that the first step in the collection process is for the IRS to actually assess the tax. Until this occurs, the IRS cannot act to collect on that tax. An assessment is simply what the IRS claims you owe. The most common forms of assessment are summary assessments and deficiency assessments.

Summary assessment will usually represent the amount reflected on a tax return that you filed, whereas a deficiency assessment can occur due to an adjustment being made to a filed tax return, such as the result of an audit, or when the IRS files a Substitute for Return.

CHAPTER 11
ILL-GOTTEN GAINS

One of our more fascinating cases began with an administrative assistant at a major industrial firm being convicted of embezzling over $200,000 from her company. She had been convicted, but in exchange for early release, she had agreed to pay back half of the money she had taken (Sounds like a good deal to me!)

After she was released and in the process of paying the money back, she received notification from the IRS that the total amount of the embezzled funds would be taxed to her as income.

She thought surely she would only be taxed on the amount that she had kept but after hiring two different attorneys, she was left holding the bag for income tax on the full amount she had taken.

You see, there is a section in the Internal Revenue Code that says that money received from an illegal source will be taxed fully as earned income.

Dang those blasted ill-gotten gains!

After losing an appeal twice with the IRS, she was referred to us by another attorney friend of hers.

She tells me her story, and I'm thinking to myself, "This one may require a little extra elbow grease!"

After she finished, she asked me what I thought. I told her first thing that I couldn't make any promises. And that we may get the exact same result as her first two tries at getting the tax thrown out.

This was going to require some serious creative thinking!

I pondered her situation for at least an hour a day for four days straight, and then it dawned on me…

If you have, say, a construction business and you build houses, your Cost of Goods Sold is your expense for the "sticks and bricks" and labor for building the house.

Similarly, I reasoned, her "expense" of paying back the money represented her deductible cost of "doing business"…never mind that it happened to be an illegal business.

So we prepared an appeal to "adjust" the tax liability that Uncle Sam was charging for her shady activities.

Our initial appeal was rejected, just like the appeals of the previous two attorneys. So we went back to the well, and kept hacking away at the problem.

Eventually… Eureka! We got a decisions in our/her favor. She would only be taxed upon the funds that she kept, and not the full amount that she had originally taken.

I'll never forget the day she received a sizeable refund check from the IRS. Close to $50,000. She was ecstatic, as you might imagine.

Yes, you read that correctly: **Refund check.**

She and her husband were very gracious for our assistance. In fact, she and her family continued as clients for the next 15 years.

CHAPTER 12

NASTY THINGS THE IRS CAN DO TO YOU: LIENS, LEVIES AND WAGE GARNISHMENTS

A Notice of Federal Tax Lien (NFTL) is an encumbrance that establishes a legal claim by the government. It does not result in the physical seizure of your property. A levy, on the other hand, allows the IRS to actually seize wages, cash, or property. Levies are normally divided into two categories. The first category includes tangible, real and personal property that you own. The second category includes third parties who hold property belonging to you such as bank deposits and wages.

The first category is often referred to as a "seizure", while the second category is usually referred to as a "levy" or "garnishment". The IRS must file a lien before they can issue a levy and must place a levy upon your property before they can seize your property. Levy action is the usually the most severe collections action the IRS takes against the majority of people that owe back taxes, and it is this type of action that an IRS employee is referring to when they talk about **"enforced collection."**

Federal Tax Liens

Once the IRS makes a valid assessment against you, the IRS is required to give notice and demand for payment within 60 days by law. If you don't pay the taxes owed, a Federal Tax Lien automatically arises and attaches to property and property rights either own directly by you or acquired after the date of the tax assessment. Both Federal law and state law are relevant in determining the effect of the Federal Tax Lien against you and your property. Federal laws determine whether the tax lien has validly attached and state law aids in determining to what property the lien attaches. Under your state laws certain property may be exempt from the lien.

In general, a tax lien gives the IRS a claim against everything you own, from your home and car all the way to the rusted bicycle in your backyard. The lien also technically attaches to your wages, money in your bank accounts, your retirement accounts, and even the cash in your wallet.

A Federal Tax Lien also impacts your credit score, since it shows up on your credit report. Therefore, the tax lien can impact your ability to obtain loans, rent an apartment, and can even impact your insurance rates and ability to obtain employment if you are a job seeker.

In most cases, a tax lien will jump ahead of many other liens against your property after a 180 day period, unless a particular piece of property is used as collateral for a loan. For example, a tax lien does not jump ahead in priority position over a car loan or a first, second, or third mortgage against your home. It will, however, usually jump ahead of, say, a mechanic's lien against your home.

You may have circumstances where having the lien released would be of benefit to helping you resolve the tax situation. There are three types of lien releases available to a taxpayer that may help you resolve tax liabilities with the IRS.

Certificate of Discharge

A Certificate of Discharge (COD) is the process of removing a single piece of property from being subject to the tax lien, usually so that the property can be legally transferred. For example, if you are trying to sell your house but the presence of the lien is preventing this from occurring, then you would need to obtain a Certificate of Discharge to release the tax lien against your house.

In the vast majority of cases, the IRS will not release a lien against a particular piece of property unless they are somehow going to benefit from it. They will generally approve a Certificate of Discharge if the lien discharge will facilitate the sale of the property in such a way that the IRS will get some money out of it. In other words, releasing the lien will facilitate collection of the tax.

If the government isn't going to see any money out of releasing a piece of property from the lien, it's possible to still obtain a Certificate of Discharge if there is a valid reason. In particular, if the IRS won't be receiving any money, but getting rid of the property will free up cash flow and put you in a better financial position in regards to your income and expenses so that later on down the road you can start paying on your taxes, then the IRS will likely approve a Certificate of Discharge.

If the property in question has no significant fair market value, the COD may also be granted, but this is much more of a hit-or-miss situation.

Lien Subordination

A lien subordination is the process of moving the tax lien down a notch in the prioritization of claims against a piece of property. For example, if you own a house free and clear, and the tax lien is in first position against the house, you can't obtain a mortgage against the house. No lender in their right mind is going to loan you money against that house unless their lien is going to take first position.

The answer to this problem is the lien subordination. The IRS will usually approve the subordination of their lien against a property if the lien that will be taking first position ahead of the tax lien will result in money going to your tax liability.

In the house example, obtaining a subordination of the tax lien in order to obtain a mortgage against the house will result in cash coming from that mortgage. At closing, that cash will go directly to the IRS, the mortgage will move into first position, and the tax lien gets re-recorded in second position.

Remember, paying interest on a loan is almost always going to be cheaper than paying penalties and interest to the IRS.

There are other conditions where a lien subordination will still be approved, even if the IRS isn't going to obtain direct proceeds from doing so. For example, many trucking companies will finance their accounts receivable through a process called factoring. In factoring, a lender pays the trucking company some percentage of their accounts receivable (usually 75% to 90%) up front, and then the lender takes the responsibility of collecting on that account receivable when it's due, usually 30 to 90 days down the road. This way, the trucking company gets money now so that they can buy fuel and make payroll.

When a tax lien is filed, most factoring lenders stop funding. In that case, the trucking company suddenly loses all its cash flow. In order to enable the funding to continue, a lien subordination can be obtained that move the tax lien to a position below the factoring lender, thereby protecting the lender's claim on those accounts receivable.

Lien Withdrawal

There are rare occasions when obtaining an outright release of the entire Federal tax lien is actually the best way to progress towards a resolution of your tax liabilities. If a case can be made that the withdrawal of the lien will facilitate payment of the tax liability, or is otherwise in the best interest of both the taxpayer and the government, then the government may be open to this.

Another case where a lien withdrawal can be applied for is when you have entered into an Installment Agreement to pay the back taxes and the agreement did not mandate that a lien be filed, particularly a payment plan where the payments are directly withdrawn from your bank account. In these cases, you can often get the lien released as long as you are current with your payments and other tax obligations.

Certificate of Release of Paid or Unenforceable Lien

The IRS is required to issue a certificate of release of lien no later than 30 days after one of the following events occur:

- The tax liability is paid in full.

- The tax liability is no longer collectible. In other words, the 10-year statute of limitations on collections has expired.

- The IRS accepts the bond of a surety company or payment of all taxes owed is to be made no later than six months before the expiration of the 10-year collection statute.

- The taxpayer delivers a cashier's check to the IRS and receives a Certificate of Release of Tax Lien.

Bank Account Levies

An IRS levy is the actual action taken by the IRS to collect past due taxes. For example, the IRS can issue a bank levy to obtain your cash in savings and checking accounts or the IRS can levy your wages or accounts receivable, if you run a business.

The person, company or institution that is served the levy must comply or face their own IRS problems. For example, when the IRS issues a levy against your bank accounts, your bank must comply. The bank is required to take the funds out of your account to which the levy attaches on the day they process the levy. They must then hold those funds for 21 days and then after the 21 days, send those funds to the IRS. If they fail to do this, the IRS will come after your bank and penalize them. The additional paperwork that the bank or other company or institution is faced with to comply with the levy usually causes your relationship to suffer with the person or institution being levied.

When a financial institution receives a levy on your bank account, it cannot surrender the money until 21 calendar days after the levy has been served. This 21-day waiting period provides you the opportunity to notify the IRS and correct any errors regarding your accounts. An extension of this 21-day period may be granted by the Area Director of the IRS if there is a legitimate dispute regarding the amount of tax owed.

Anytime during the 21-day waiting period the levy can be released. During these 21 days it is imperative that you exercise your appeals rights. In this case, you will want to file a CAP appeal. CAP stands for Collection Appeals Process. When you file a CAP appeal, the IRS must hear your case within five days. Please see the chapter on Appeals for more information about this process.

Levies should be avoided at all costs and are usually the result of poor communication with your Revenue Officer. When the IRS levies a bank account, the levy is only for the particular day the levy is received by the bank. As I mentioned, the bank is required to remove whatever amount of money is available in your account that day up to the maximum amount of the IRS levy and send it to the IRS after that 21 day hold period. This type of levy does not affect future deposits. So if your bank account gets levied today and all the money is taken out by the bank to be sent to the IRS 21 days later, you can make a deposit tomorrow that is not subject to that IRS levy.

An IRS wage levy is quite different. Wage levies are filed with your employer and remain in effect until the IRS notifies the employer that the wage levy has been released. Most wage levies take so much money from your paycheck that you don't have enough money to live on. In most circumstances, an IRS wage garnishment will take 70% to 80% of your entire paycheck. For most taxpayers, wage garnishments are the worst thing the IRS can do to them, and everything possible should be done to avoid this debilitating attack on your personal finances.

Personal Property Levies

The IRS's levy power is extremely broad and does not require that the IRS take you to court. The IRS can use its authority to gain possession of your property to pay any back taxes owed and all they have to do is file a notice in demand of payment, wait 10 days, then file a 30-day notice of intent to levy. After that 30 days, they can then levy. The effect of a levy is to compel you to turn property over to the IRS. Amounts that the IRS gains from a levy or garnishment are applied to your tax debt as follows:

1. The proceeds are applied to the expenses of the levy in sale.
2. Proceeds from the levy are then applied to the tax specifically relating to the levied property.

3. Proceeds are then applied to the delinquent tax liability that caused the whole situation in the first place.

4. Funds collected by a levy are considered to have been paid involuntarily. Therefore, you cannot specify to the IRS how you want those funds applied, which you are normally able to do if you make voluntary payments. This is yet another reason why levies are best avoided.

As we already mentioned, the IRS is required to notify you of its intent to levy you at least 30 days before the levy. This is done thru a notice called a Letter 1058 and states across the top of the notice, "Final Notice of Intent to Levy". When you are issued a Letter 1058 by the IRS, you have broad appeals right that allows you to appeal the proposed action. However, your appeal must be submitted within the 30 day window. If you've recently receive a final notice of intent to levy, please see the Chapter on Appeals to learn how to file a Collection Due Process appeal.

Seizures

The IRS must issue a notice of seizure to the owner of any real property (e.g. real estate) or the possessor of personal property as soon as practicable after the property is seized. This notice has the same effect as the Notice of Levy and can be delivered in person to the owner or possessor of the property or left at your home or normal place of business. Seizures must always be approved by upper IRS management. The supervisor must review your information, verify that the balance is due and affirm that a lien, levy or seizure is appropriate under the circumstances. Failure to give the proper notice will invalidate the seizure and afford you certain legal rights.

Seizures of your residence or business

The IRS is no longer really in the business of seizing homes and entire businesses. These sorts of seizures have become relatively infrequent, largely in due to the adverse publicity that the IRS has received from conducting these actions. The Taxpayer Bill of Rights prohibits the IRS from seizing real property that is used as a residence by the taxpayer for tax amounts of $5,000 or less, including penalties and interest. The Taxpayer Bill of Rights also only permits a levy or seizure on a principal residence if a judge approves of the seizure in writing. Following the 1998 Restructuring Amendments to the Internal Revenue Code, the process for seizing your home has become incredibly difficult for the IRS, which is a good thing for you.

Wage Garnishments

The IRS wage garnishment is a very powerful tool used to collect taxes owed by bringing your employer into the situation. A wage garnishment cannot only be an inconvenience and an embarrassment but it can also leave you with no money to pay your regular living expenses. Once a wage garnishment is filed with your employer, the employer is required to collect the vast majority of each of your paychecks and send that money to the IRS. As mentioned earlier, the wage garnishment will usually take 70% to 80% of your paycheck. In addition, if you receive Social Security, the IRS can take up to 15% of each and every one of your Social Security checks. The wage garnishment stays in effect until either the IRS is paid or the IRS agrees to release the garnishment.

A wage garnishment can be appealed through the Collection Appeals Program, just like a bank account levy. In addition, wage garnishments are a situation where seeking assistance from the Taxpayer Advocate can be extremely helpful.

Fair Debt Collection Practices Act

The IRS is subject to the conditions of the Fair Debt Collection Practices Act just like any other debt collector. This Act includes a number of rules controlling debt collection practices. Normally, these rules are to prevent excessive collections practices from being undertaken by collection agencies for things such as credit card debts and automobile payments. However, the Taxpayer Bill of Rights follows the Fair Debt Collection Practices Act guidelines and provides you certain rights.

For example, you cannot be contacted by a Collections Representative of the IRS outside of the hours of 8AM to 9PM, and it also prohibits harassing or abusive behavior from the IRS to you. The IRS may not communicate with you at an unusual time or place which is known or which should be known to be inconvenient to you. The IRS can also not communicate with you regarding your tax liability at your place of employment if the IRS knows or has reason to know that your employer prohibits you from receiving such communication.

If the IRS knows that you are represented by someone who is authorized to practice before the IRS, then they can also not contact you. This provision does not apply if your power of attorney representative does not respond to the IRS within a reasonable period of time after being requested to do so. That is why it's important that if you hire professional tax resolution representation that you hire a reputable firm that's going to actually do what you pay them to do.

Tax Resolution Resource

A skilled representative relieves stress, and offers you the best protection from the IRS. <u>We become your IRS shield.</u>

If you have anxiety when speaking directly to the IRS, please feel free to call us: **(770) 984-8008**.

As a thank you for reading our book we'll give you a **FREE Tax Debt Settlement Analysis**. You can then decide quickly if we will be the right shield for you.

CHAPTER 13

MY FAVORITE CLIENT, EVERETT SUTERS

Everett Suters was the head of a well-known publishing company based in Atlanta. Additionally, he had numerous other highly successful business ventures right up to his passing in 2015.

He was quite well-known, even internationally, and I actually knew of him before we met. When he first came into our office in the late 1990's, he and his publishing business were reeling financially.

He had just become the victim of embezzlement amounting to several hundred thousand dollars.

Everett had received a call from his banker one morning, who sheepishly told him that there were several checks being presented against his account, but that his balance had gone well into overdraft status.

Everett recounted the conversation with his banker, telling how the six-figure amount he was expecting to be in the account was for payroll taxes owed to the IRS.

He didn't hire us that day. He told me instead, he was interviewing another CPA and two other attorneys before deciding who he wanted to represent him, now that the IRS wanted the payroll taxes that were owed to them of over $650,000.

We didn't hear from him for three weeks, and I assumed he had chosen one of my esteemed colleagues to represent him against the IRS.

And then finally, he called and made an appointment, and said he wanted us to take his case.

While our first meeting was certainly pleasant, our second meeting was considerably more relaxed. Since he had told me we were one of four firms he was considering, I asked him how it was he had decided on us.

I was heartened by his response. He said that he we had taken much more interest in him personally and in the facts of his case by far more than the other three firms. He said he had felt very much at ease, both with me and with the others in our office. Interestingly, he also said we seemed more creative than the others he had interviewed.

At the end of our first visit, I had given him a copy of my very first book, *On Level Ground with the IRS*. So lastly, he said it definitely helped to be able to hire "the guy that literally wrote the book" on dealing with IRS problems!

Over the weeks and months ahead, we talked or met probably a dozen times, which is considerably more than usual.

He invited me to lunch a couple of times, and before long he knew everybody in our office, and also who all my family members were. He even knew what was going on with each.

The "Reader's Digest" version of his IRS case was that we were successful in getting the IRS to accept our Offer in Compromise for just over $65,000, or about ten percent of what he owed then— before adding penalties and interest.

He was extremely happy, and so were we.

The lunch invitations continued.

Some of our lunches would run three or more hours. It was not at all unusual for people to come greet him at lunch, even strangers. Without exception, he was always gracious and spent time with each person that greeted him.

Everett was extremely well-known around the world for his marketing and management expertise. Before long, he began offering guidance to me during our lunch meetings, on how to use various marketing strategies to grow our practice.

He was obviously very pleased over the settlement we were able to reach for him with the IRS and from then on, he hired our firm to handle all tax matters and issues for his several businesses and all of his family matters.

That was in the late 1990's. Throughout the 2000's, he was much more a friend and mentor than a client.

We talked for hours about personal, deep stuff that I didn't get into with any of our other clients, whether local or thousands of miles away.

In December, 2014, our younger daughter, Kimberly, was married, and we asked Everett and his lovely wife, Gary, to join us at the reception as special guests at our table. It was an honor for us to have them there to share in this experience.

We were fortunate to get an exceptional result for Everett. But that wasn't what made him exceptional.

I could easily enumerate a long list of the special attributes that went together to make Everett Suters a very special individual.

Due to space limitations, I'll just name one:

He was an incredible friend to my family and to our office team. And these weren't the gratuitous inquiries of a salesman trying to close a deal. He didn't have anything to sell me.

He was genuinely interested in the people that were in my life. My wife, Robin, had a sister that was stricken with muscular dystrophy. When her health began to decline, he asked about her constantly, up to the time of her death.

Every person should be so blessed to have caring friends like Everett Suters and his dear, gracious wife, Gary, in their lives.

He just genuinely cared about people, even new acquaintances, as if somehow it were his calling. Perhaps it was.

Rest in peace, my dear friend.

CHAPTER 14

"REGRETS, I'VE HAD FEW…"

If you are anywhere from 40 to 70 years of age, you'll recognize this phrase from the Frank Sinatra standard, "My Way".

Of all things, I recently learned that my daughter, Katherine, and her husband, Stephen, have both become fans of the Rat Pack! (Who was it—Sinatra, Dean Martin, and Sammy Davis Jr.?)

I've heard it said that in life, at least over the long term, we regret the things that we didn't do much more than those misguided things that we did do.

If you've hung with me to this final chapter, hopefully you have discovered a valuable treasure chest of tax secrets. Both for putting your IRS problems behind you, and also for cutting your future income taxes.

More money for you. Legally and ethically!

Did you realize that taxes are our number one living expense? They consume more of our income than our cost of housing, meals, and clothing… Combined!

Throughout this book I have attempted to give you a "safety net", of sorts, so that you can sleep tonight knowing that your IRS problem does have a solution.

Yet at the same time, <u>knowing there is a solution but not pursuing it is little better than not knowing that the solution exists</u>.

If you have a severe health issue, you seek out a healthcare specialist who will prescribe a course of action to correct your condition. But that prescription, whether it be for a course of medication or major surgery, won't help you if you don't follow the steps prescribed.

All of us in life have regrets over things we have done.

You may not be ready to take control of your tax and financial life. You may be perfectly happy to stay where you are right now. And that's fine.

If life has handed you a difficult tax or financial situation, don't waste time kicking yourself.

It's not your fault!

The IRS wants to keep you right where you are, overpaying your taxes and covered up with more penalties and interest than you could ever escape from on your own.

They would love to keep you in the deep hole that life has pushed you into.

You can either claw with all of your might, trying unsuccessfully to get a foothold…

Or you can give up and just hope for the best…

Or, you can take hold of the ladder that we have just lowered to you in the preceding chapters, and comfortably take the first step… Then the second.

Are you ready to take the first step towards regaining financial control of your life?

We would love to hear from you! Give us a call today at **(770) 984-8008.**

About The Author

Dennis Bridges is a CPA, currently celebrating 30 years in practice. His office is based in Atlanta, but he and his team assist clients throughout the U.S. His practice focuses on tax preparation, tax-cutting strategies, and IRS representation for a variety of industries and professions including:

- Trucking and transportation
- Healthcare, especially nursing
- Attorneys and judiciary
- Construction
- Home-based businesses and direct marketers
- Law enforcement, for sworn officers at Federal, State, and Local levels

He is a recognized leader in the resolution of severe IRS and state tax issues for all taxpayers. He and his team have assisted taxpayers in all fifty states.

He has spoken to industry groups throughout the country, and has addressed national conferences of attorneys and CPAs in Denver, Las Vegas, and Chicago.

Dennis's articles have been published dozens of times in industry periodicals as well as professional journals. He is the author of *On Level Ground with the IRS*, and is a contributor to the best-selling tax guide, *Breaking the Tax Code, 2nd Ed.*

Dennis and his wife, Robin, have two grown daughters, Katherine and Kimberly. They are now empty-nesters, except for three cats that pretty much control their lives.

To learn more about Dennis and his firm, visit http://CPAofAtlanta.com or call **(770) 984-8008** to schedule an appointment.

www.ingramcontent.com/pod-product-compliance
Lightning Source LLC
Chambersburg PA
CBHW071821200526
45169CB00018B/504